**TRAVERSE**
THEATRE

Traverse Theatre Company

# Outlying Islands

## by David Greig

### Cast in order of appearance

| | |
|---|---|
| *Robert* | Laurence Mitchell |
| *John* | Sam Heughan |
| *Kirk* | Robert Carr |
| *Ellen* | Lesley Hart |
| *Captain* | Robert Carr |

| | |
|---|---|
| Director | Philip Howard |
| Designer | Fiona Watt |
| Lighting designer | Chahine Yavroyan |
| Composer | Gavin Marwick |
| Assistant director | Helen-Marie O'Malley |
| Stage manager | Gavin Harding |
| Deputy stage manager | Brendan Graham |
| Assistant stage manager | Gemma Smith |
| Wardrobe supervisor | Lynn Ferguson |
| Wardrobe assistant | Stephanie Thorburn |

**First performed at the Traverse Theatre**
**Friday 12 July 2002**

# TRAVERSE THEATRE

**powerhouse of new writing** DAILY TELEGRAPH

### Artistic Director Philip Howard

The Traverse is Scotland's new writing theatre. Founded in 1963 by a group of maverick artists and enthusiasts, it began as an imaginative attempt to capture the spirit of adventure and experimentation of the Edinburgh Festival all year round. Throughout the decades, the Traverse has evolved and grown in artistic output and ambition. It has refined its mission by strengthening its commitment to producing new plays by Scottish and international playwrights and actively nurturing them throughout their careers. Traverse productions have been seen world wide and tour regularly throughout the UK and overseas.

The Traverse has produced over 600 new plays in its lifetime and, through a spirit of innovation and risk-taking, has launched the careers of many of the country's best known writers. From, among others, Stanley Eveling in the 1960s, John Byrne in the 1970s, Liz Lochhead in the 1980s, David Greig in the 1990s to Gregory Burke in the 2000s, the Traverse is unique in Scotland in its dedication to new writing. It fulfils the crucial role of providing the infrastructure, professional support and expertise to ensure the development of a dynamic theatre culture for Scotland.

The Traverse's activities encompass every aspect of playwriting and production, providing and facilitating play reading panels, script development workshops, rehearsed readings, public playwriting workshops, writers groups, a public playwrights platform, The Monday Lizard, discussions and special events. The Traverse's work with young people is of supreme importance and takes the form of encouraging playwriting through its flagship education project, Class Act, as well as the Traverse Young Writers Group.

**Edinburgh's Traverse Theatre is a mini-festival in itself** THE TIMES

From its conception in the 1960s, the Traverse has remained a pivotal venue during the Edinburgh Festival. It receives enormous critical and audience acclaim for its programming, as well as regularly winning awards. The year 2001 was no different with the Traverse being awarded two Scotsman Fringe Firsts and two Herald Angels for its own productions Gagarin Way and Wiping My Mother's Arse and a Herald Archangel for overall artistic excellence.

For further information on the Traverse Theatre's activities and history, an online resource is available at www.virtualtraverse.com. To find out about ways to support the Traverse, please contact Jayne Gross, Development Manager on 0131 228 3223.

# COMPANY BIOGRAPHIES

**Robert Carr** (*Kirk, Captain*) For the Traverse: KING OF THE FIELDS and SOLEMN MASS FOR A FULL MOON IN SUMMER. Other recent theatre work includes LOSING ALEC (Cumbernauld Theatre), STIFF! (Diva Productions), DEAD FUNNY, KIDNAPPED, CARLUCCO AND THE QUEEN OF HEARTS, MARY QUEEN OF SCOTS GOT HER HEAD CHOPPED OFF, TRAVESTIES, MIRANDOLINA, THE MARRIAGE OF FIGARO (Royal Lyceum), GONE FISHING, A SATIRE OF THE FOUR ESTAITES, NO EXPENSE SPARED (Wildcat), DUMBSTRUCK (Tron), THE BARBER OF SEVILLE (Arches). Film and TV includes Johnston, the Goat Farmer in MONARCH OF THE GLEN, Mr Leitch in ORPHANS, Haldene in THE CREATIVES, THE BALDY MAN, TAGGART, Harry MacLiesh in HAMISH MACBETH and Ferret in THE HIGH LIFE.

**David Greig** (Writer) was born in Edinburgh. His previous works for the Traverse include THE SPECULATOR, DANNY 306+ME FOREVER, THE ARCHITECT and EUROPE. Other theatre works include CASANOVA, ONE WAY STREET, AIRPORT, TIMELESS, MAINSTREAM (Suspect Culture), THE COSMONAUT'S LAST MESSAGE TO THE WOMAN HE ONCE LOVED IN A FORMER SOVIET UNION (Tron), DR KORCZAK'S EXAMPLE (TAG Theatre Company) and VICTORIA (RSC). He has written a number of radio plays for BBC Radio and is currently working on a full-length feature film for Kudos.

**Lesley Hart** (*Ellen*) Trained at the RSAMD. For the Traverse: AMONG UNBROKEN HEARTS (Highland Tour 2000; Bush Theatre, London 2001), SHETLAND SAGA. Other theatre work includes: RUNNING GIRL (Boilerhouse), A MIDSUMMER NIGHTS DREAM, THE TWITS (Citizens).

**Sam Heughan** (*John*) is currently in his second year at RSAMD. College productions include: ROMEO AND JULIET, PROMETHEUS BOUND, CRIME AND PUNISHMENT, THE SEAGULL. Other theatre includes: THE TWITS (Citizens), MACBETH, SHERLOCK HOMES (Edinburgh Festivals 2000-2001). Film credits include SMALL MOMENTS (Short Film Factory). Former Lyceum Youth Theatre member. Recently won the Elaine Campbell Gullen Trophy for verse speaking and joint winner of the Duncan MacRae Memorial Prize for Scots Speaking 2002.

**Philip Howard** (Director): Philip trained at the Royal Court Theatre, London, on the Regional Theatre Young Director Scheme from 1988-90. He was Associate Director at the Traverse from 1993-96, and has been Artistic Director since 1996. Productions for the Traverse include: LOOSE

ENDS, BROTHERS OF THUNDER, EUROPE, KNIVES IN HENS (also The Bush Theatre), THE ARCHITECT, FAITH HEALER, WORMWOOD, LAZYBED, THE CHIC NERDS, KILL THE OLD TORTURE THEIR YOUNG, HERITAGE (1998 & 2001), THE SPECULATOR, HIGHLAND SHORTS, SOLEMN MASS FOR A FULL MOON IN SUMMER (with Ros Steen), SHETLAND SAGA, THE TRESTLE AT POPE LICK CREEK, WIPING MY MOTHER'S ARSE and THE BALLAD OF CRAZY PAOLA. Philip's other theatre work includes HIPPOLYTUS (Arts Theatre Cambridge), ENTERTAINING MR SLOANE (Royal, Northampton) and SOMETHING ABOUT US (Lyric Hammersmith Studio).

**Gavin Marwick** (Composer): Born Edinburgh. Founder member of and composer with IRON HORSE, a contemporary traditional band which has toured over four continents and released five albums. Gavin also plays with Jonny Hardie (of OLD BLIND DOGS) in fiddle duo UP IN THE AIR. For the Traverse: THE TRESTLE AT POPE LICK CREEK, HERITAGE, FAITH HEALER, HIGHLAND SHORTS. For the BBC: THE GAME KEEPER. Discography: THE IRON HORSE, THRO WATER EARTH AND STONE, FIVE HANDS HIGH, VOICE OF THE LAND, DEMONS AND LOVERS (all for IRON HORSE), UP IN THE AIR (with Jonny Hardie), THE WEIRD SET (with BURACH), CEILIDH SETS (with the MARWICKS).

**Laurence Mitchell** (*Robert*) Trained at the Drama Centre. Theatre work includes: FREE (National Theatre), TIME AND THE CONWAYS (Royal Exchange), AFORE NIGHT COME (Young Vic), ACCOMPLICES, MR ENGLAND (RNT Studio - Sheffield Theatre co-productions), SIX DEGREES OF SEPARATION (Crucible Theatre), TROILUS & CRESSIDA (Oxford Stage Company), NEVER THE SINNER (Library Theatre, Manchester), FILUMENA (Peter Hall Company at the Piccadilly), THE DOCTOR'S DILEMMA (Almeida), CAUSE CELEBRE (Lyric, Hammersmith). His television work includes KAVANAGH QC.

**Helen-Marie O'Malley** (Assistant Director) Trained at the RSAMD. For the Traverse: FIRST BITE 2002; COLD COME CRANES GONE. Assistant Director on: THE BALLAD OF CRAZY PAOLA; FIRST BITE 2001; HERITAGE; THE TRESTLE AT POPE LICK CREEK and GREEN FIELD. Other Theatre work includes: SLEEPING AROUND (Tron); AND THEN THERE WERE NONE (Fonts). Directing and Performing: NIGHT SKY, NO MOON; NO STARS (Wisconsin, USA). Helen-Marie is a winner of both the Bruce Millar and a recipient of the John Fernald Awards for directors

**Fiona Watt** (Designer) Trained: Motley (Almeida). Awarded Arts Council Resident Design Bursary 1996 (Wolsey, Ipswich). For the Traverse: HIGHLAND SHORTS, HERITAGE. Other theatre includes: THE BOOK OF MIRACLES (Nottingham Roundabout); SANCTUARY (Yorkshire Women); JULIUS CAESAR (TAG), OUTWARD BOUND, LOVE BITES (Palace Theatre, Watford); A WALK ON LAKE ERIE (Finborough); GRACE IN AMERICA (Old Red Lion). Opera: LA PIETRA DEL PARAGONE, GIANNI SCHICCHI (RSAMD), LA TRAVIATA (Haddo), MAVRA, RIDERS TO THE SEA. Film: NITRATE WON'T WAIT (First Reels). Exhibition: TIME & SPACE (RCA, London), THEATRE DESIGN at the Tron as part of the UK City of Architecture & Design and 2D>>3D (Sheffield Galleries, Autumn 2002).

**Chahine Yavroyan** (Lighting Designer): Trained at the Bristol Old Vic Theatre School. For the Traverse: GREEN FIELD, GAGARIN WAY; WIPING MY MOTHER'S ARSE; KING OF THE FIELDS, THE SPECULATOR, DANNY 306 + ME (4 EVER), PERFECT DAYS, KILL THE OLD TORTURE THEIR YOUNG, ANNA WEISS, KNIVES IN HENS, THE ARCHITECT AND SHINING SOULS. He has worked extensively in theatre, with companies and artists including: Crucible, Royal Court, Nottingham Playhouse, Leicester Haymarket, ICA, ENO, Lindsay Kemp, Rose English, Pip Simmons. Dance work includes: Yolande Snaith Theatredance, Bock & Vincenzi, Anatomy Performance Company, Naheed Saddiqui. Chahine has also worked on many site specific works including Station House Opera, Dreamwork at St Pancras Chambers, Coin St Museum, City of Bologna, Italy New Year's Eve celebrations. Fashion shows for Givenchy, Chalayan, Clemens-Riberio, Ghost. He is also a long standing People Show Person.

**The Traverse Trivia Quiz in association with Tennents**

**with thanks to: Navy Blue Design Consultants
and Stewarts, graphic designers and printers
for the Traverse**

**Arts & Business
for management and mentoring services**

**Purchase of the Traverse Box Office,
computer network and technical and training
equipment has been made possible with money
from The Scottish Arts Council National Lottery Fund**

Scottish
**Arts** Council
LOTTERY FUNDED

**The Traverse Theatre's work would not be possible
without the support of**

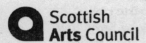 

Scottish
**Arts** Council

·EDINBVRGH·
THE CITY OF EDINBURGH COUNCIL

**The Traverse receives financial assistance for its
educational and development work from**

Calouste Gulbenkian Foundation, John Lewis Partnership, Peggy
Ramsay Foundation, Binks Trust, The Bulldog Prinsep Theatrical
Trust, Esmee Fairbairn Trust, Gannochy Trust, Gordon Fraser
Charitable Trust, JSP Pollitzer Charitable Trust, The Hope Trust,
The Steel Trust, Paul Hamlyn Foundation, The Craignish Trust,
Lindsay's Charitable Trust, Tay Charitable Trust, Ernest Cook Trust,
Sir John Fisher Foundation, Hanns and Elizabeth Rausing
Charitable Trust

Charity No. SC002368

**For their generous help on
OUTLYING ISLANDS
the Traverse thanks**

everyone who kindly assisted
in the making of this production

Royal Lyceum Theatre
for wardrobe assistance

Sets, props and costumes for
OUTLYING ISLANDS
created by Traverse Workshops
(funded by the National Lottery)

 Scottish
Arts Council
LOTTERY FUNDED

Costume maker Jackie Holt
Production photography by Kevin Low
Print photography by Euan Myles

**For their continued generous support
of Traverse productions we thank**

**Habitat**

**Marks and Spencer, Princes Street**

**Camerabase**

**BHS**

# TRAVERSE THEATRE - THE COMPANY

| | |
|---|---|
| Gillian Adams | Second Chef |
| Jeremy Adderley | Bar Café Manager |
| Louise Anderson | Marketing & Press Assistant |
| Paul Axford | Corporate Development Co-ordinator |
| Maria Bechaalani | Deputy Electrician |
| Stuart Cargill | Assistant Chef |
| Andy Catlin | Marketing Manager |
| Mary Charleton | Artistic Administrator (Maternity cover) |
| David Connell | Finance Manager |
| Neil Coull | Literary Assistant |
| Andrew Coulton | Assistant Electrician |
| Eric Dickinson | Kitchen Assistant |
| Jude Durnan | Deputy Box Office Manager |
| Lynn Ferguson | Wardrobe Supervisor |
| Michael Fraser | Theatre Manager |
| David Freeburn | Box Office Manager |
| Riccardo Galgani | Pearson Playwright in Residence |
| Susie Gray | Press & Marketing Officer |
| Mike Griffiths | Administrative Director |
| Jayne Gross | Development Manager |
| Kellie Harris | Head Chef |
| Philip Howard | Artistic Director |
| Nathan Huxtable | Senior Bar Cafe Attendant |
| Hal Jones | Carpenter |
| Kevin McCune | Assistant Bar Café Manager |
| Lara McDonald | Administrative Assistant |
| Stewart McDonald | Head Bar Person |
| Chris McDougall | Technical Stage Manager |
| Catherine Macneil | Artistic Administrator |
| Katherine Mendelsohn | International Literary Associate |
| Nick Millar | Production Manager |
| Kate Nelson | Monday Lizard Co-ordinator |
| Duncan Nicoll | Deputy Bar Café Manager |
| Helen-Marie O'Malley | Assistant Director |
| Pauleen Rafferty | Finance & Personnel Assistant |
| Renny Robertson | Chief Electrician |
| Hannah Rye | Literary Development Officer |
| Roxana Silbert | Literary Director |
| Zoe Squair | Front of House Manager |
| Stephanie Thorburn | Wardrobe Assistant |
| Isabel Wright | Associate Playwright |

## Also working for the Traverse

Ewan Anderson, Marianne Barr, Nancy Birch, Kenny Brodie, Leo Buckingham, Alex Bynoth, Vanessa Cassey, Paul Claydon, Anna Copland, Annie Divine, Jenny Duttine, Mary Ellis, Beccy Finch, Vikki Graves, Linda Gunn, Malcolm Hamilton, Sinead Harvey, Chris Jones, Linda Keys, Brooke Laing, Kate Leiper, Jemima Levick, Jon Ley, Amy Logan, John Lyndon, Euan McDonald, Hollie McDonald, Donna McGlynn, Anna MacInnes, James Miller, Paul Nowak, Clare Padgett, Dominic Rafferty, Jennifer Reader, Naomi Schwock, Alistair Stott, Centli Templeton, Mark Thomson, Joe Vernon.

## TRAVERSE THEATRE BOARD OF DIRECTORS

Stuart Hepburn (Chair), Kate Atkinson, Roy Campbell, Steven Cotton, Leslie Evans, Geraldine Gammell, Robin Harper MSP, Christine Hamilton, John Stone, Stuart Murray (Company Secretary) Keith Welch.

# David Greig
# Outlying Islands

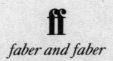

*faber and faber*

First published in 2002
by Faber and Faber Limited
3 Queen Square, London WC1N 3AU

Typeset by Country Setting, Kingsdown, Kent CT14 8ES
Printed in England by Mackays of Chatham plc, Chatham, Kent

A CIP record for this book
is available from the British Library

ISBN 0–571–21760–5

2 4 6 8 10 9 7 5 3

# For Rory

# Acknowledgements

With grateful thanks to Catherine Bailey Ltd,
without whose support this play could not
have been written.

I would also like to thank the following people for
their help, support and advice during the writing
of *Outlying Islands*:

Marilyn Imrie, Louise Ludgate, William Houston,
Oliver Milburn, Sean Scanlan, Stuart McQuarrie,
David Harrower, Katherine Mendelsohn and,
as always, Mel Kenyon.

Heartfelt thanks for this and so many other plays
go to Davey, Nathan, Katherine, Vanessa and
all the staff of the Traverse Bar for putting up
with me so kindly, feeding me espressos
while I sat in the corner.

*Although the depiction of the characters and the
story of the play are entirely the playwright's fiction,
David Greig and the Traverse Theatre gratefully
acknowledge* Island Going *by Robert Atkinson
(Birlinn, 1995) as the inspiration and starting point
for the play.*

# Characters

**Kirk**
tacksman of the island

**Ellen**
Kirk's neice

**John**
a naturalist

**Robert**
a naturalist

**The Captain**

*Setting*

A small island in the North Atlantic
in the summer months before the Second World War

## ONE

*The sound of water on a shore.*

**Robert** I have noticed that something draws us towards
outlying islands. Some force pulls. A quiet bay, an island
in its middle – we take a small boat and we row out
from the land. We circle the island, looking for a beach.
We pull up the boat and light cigarettes. We walk the
island's boundaries. We make a fire.
    We sit on the beach and drink beer.
    We cast our eyes back to the far shore from which
we've come.
    Night falls and the mainland slips into darkness.
    We listen to the waves.
    The island claims us.

    *The crash of the sea on rocks.*
       *A cliff.*
       *A thousand seabirds.*

I have noticed from the study of maps.
    The more outlying the island –
    The further out it is in the remote ocean –
    The stronger the force that pulls us towards it.


TWO

*On an outlying island.*
    *In the chapel.*
    *The chapel is a roughly built stone building, half
underground, with a roof of turf. Once it was a
primitive church for the small community that occupied*

*the island. For a hundred years now it has only been
occupied once a summer by mainland shepherds.*
    *Late afternoon.*
    *John outside, struggling to open the door.*

**John** Mr Kirk – I can't seem to –
    The door won't budge. The stones must have shifted
during the winter. It's stuck fast.

**Kirk** Force it.

    *John tries to open the door.*

Give it a kick, boy.

**John** What – just . . .?

**Kirk** Kick it.

    *A kick.*

Harder boy.

    *A harder kick.*

Take a run at it.

    *Pause.*

    *John hurls his full weight at the door.*
        *He grunts with effort.*
        *The door-frame cracks and splinters. The door falls.*
        *John crashes to the floor.*

**John** We're in.
    Oww.
    I think I might have done something to my shoulder.
    I can't see a bloody thing, excuse my French.

    *John lights a match.*

Good God.
    What a mess.
    Some of your sheep must have got in over winter.

**Kirk**  It's a roof.

**John**  It's – it's perfect. Ideal. Table. Fireplace. We can lay out the sleeping bags over there.
    A lamp.
    Does it work?

**Kirk**  Try it.

*John lights the paraffin lamp.*
    *The chapel is illuminated.*

**John**  Light.

**Kirk**  That door's broke.
    Took me best part of two days last annual to fix up that door.
    Now it's broke.
    I'll need compensated for that.

**John**  It doesn't look too bad.

**Kirk**  According to my letter the ministry are liable for any losses incurred during the course of your survey. Would that be right, now?

**John**  Of course.

**Kirk**  There is an inventory of goods, sir.
    It is all to be accounted for.
    I'll need to claim now for the work and the materials.
    To the cost of one door.

**John**  It was stuck. I don't want to pick nits, Mr Kirk, but there was no other way of entering the property.

**Kirk**  It was stuck.
    But if you ministry boys weren't come to my island –
to make your studies of the birds –
    No one would be wishing to open it.
    So, sir, you could say –
    It was a door serving its purpose.
    Until your arrival.

**John**  Perhaps I did take a bit too much of a run at it.
Still.
We'll need to repair it as soon as we can, anyway.
Against the weather.

**Kirk**  You'll be using peats for the fire, I take it.
From the peat store.

**John**  We're only staying for a month.

**Kirk**  And there will be disruption to the sheep.

**John**  What?

**Kirk**  They're easily disturbed.

**John**  By what?

**Kirk**  Human presence. They see no people most of the year.

**John**  They see you – once a summer.

**Kirk**  They know me.
I am a friendly face.

**John**  Mr Kirk, I don't have any power in these matters.
If you talk to the right official –
I'm sure he'll see you're fully compensated.
Right.
I'll go and see where Robert's got to with the rest of the kit.
We'll get ourselves set up in here.

**Kirk**  My niece and myself will be sleeping in the shepherd's bothy.

**John**  Right.

**Kirk**  I'll take the table now if you want.

**John**  Table? Oh – but we'll need the table to work.

**Kirk**  There was no mention of your needing a table.

**John** We need to write up our notes and develop photographs and so on.

**Kirk** The island has no other table.

**John** I see.

**Kirk** At what are we to eat?

**John** You could eat with us. We'll all eat together. At the table.

**Kirk** I wouldn't want to disturb your work.

**John** Of course.
You must.
I mean – I wouldn't have it any other way.

**Kirk** If I'd been informed about the need of a table.
I could have brought one on the boat.

**John** No. No.
It's quite all right. We'll eat together.
Simple fare. But –
We didn't come here expecting a grand hotel, Mr Kirk.
Robert and I –
This is perfect.
Ideal.

**Kirk** This was their chapel – if you can call it a chapel.
The last people.
It gives me no pleasure to eat amongst their stoor,
even for a month only.
But it has the table and the hearth.
It will suffice for the purpose.

**John** Amazing, isn't it, to think that a hundred years ago there were people who actually lived here.

**Kirk** They were pagans. It is a pagan place.
Make yourself at home.

*Kirk exits.*

**John** Right.
Jesus, it stinks in here.
Right.

*Wind.*
*John tries to shut the door.*
*He succeeds, partially.*
*Quiet.*

Fire.
Right ho.
Fire . . .
Peats.
. . .
Jesus, dark as the buggering grave.

*Lights a match again.*

No tinder.

*Tries to strike a match.*
*Fails.*

**John** Damp. Right. Damp. So.

*From outside, the arrival of Robert, out of breath and shivering.*

**Robert** Johnny. Johnny. Have you seen the cliffs yet?

**John** The door's stuck.

*Robert tries to open the door.*
*Fails.*

Hold on, I'll –

*Robert kicks the door.*

**Robert** Let us in, Johnny, I'm freezing.

**John** I'll just give it a tug here –

*Robert runs at and shoulder-barges the door.*

14

*He knocks John down under the door and falls
himself into a heap on the floor.*

**John** Oww.

**Robert** Stinks in here. Smell of bird. Fulmar oil.
Can't see a thing.

**John** God.
Can you just –
You're on top of me, old bean.

*Robert gets up. His eyes adjust.*

**Robert** This is perfect. Perfect. The village chapel. The
stink. Hasn't been occupied for years. The shepherds use
the bothy, you see. Kirk told me on the boat – they won't
sleep in the chapel. Stones must have shifted in the
winter. What are you doing on the floor?

**John** Nothing. Just – well – I was pushed over. You
pushed me over.
Where's the kit?

**Robert** On the beach.

**John** What?

**Robert** I went exploring.

**John** You're wet.
It's not raining is it?

**Robert** I went for a swim.
At the the cliff bottom, there's a rock stack, about
twenty yards offshore.
It looked inviting.

**John** Wasn't it cold?

**Robert** Burning cold.
At first your nerves don't feel it. You're numb.
Until you climb out.

And it hits you like a whip.
Took the breath right out of me.
You should come.

**John** You'll catch your death.

**Robert** I've never felt more alive. I promise you.

**John** There's weather coming, Robert, we need the kit in.
And we'll need to fix up the door.
The old man wants to write to the ministry for
compensation.

**Robert** We're a long way from the ministry now.

**John** Let's just fix the door before you freeze to death.

**Robert** You could have got the fire on.

**John** No tinder.

**Robert** What's this? Paraffin. Drop of that'll soon get us
started.

*He unscrews the lid from the paraffin bottle.*
*He pours the liquid on the peats.*

**John** The matches are damp.
The sea must have got in on the crossing.
There's dry matches with the kit.

**Robert** The cliffs, John – you must see them – the noise
of them. Kittiwakes, guillemots, razorbills, puffins,
fulmars, shags . . .

**John** I know.

**Robert** No sign of the fork-tails. I was hoping for a
glimpse of one.

**John** They're here. We've a whole month to study them.
And we're not even unpacked yet.

**Robert**  Here we go.
  Fire.
  I've got a cigarette lighter.

**John**  Wait, Robert – you just poured.

  *The cigarette lighter is lit.*
    *An explosion.*
    *The two boys knocked backwards.*
    *Pause.*

**John**  Paraffin.

**Robert**  Gosh.

**John**  Half a gallon.

**Robert**  I smell burning hair.

**John**  Yes.

**Robert**  I've never smelt that before.

**John**  You blew us up.

**Robert**  Hair and skin burned.

**John**  Yes.
  Oww.

**Robert**  Sudden light, then a sucking of air, an engulfing roar, the sound of a flame taking but amplified to a factor of what?

**John**  My shoulder hurts.

**Robert**  Would you say thirty? A factor of thirty. Absolute clarity of vision for a second then we go backwards, but we weren't knocked backwards.

**John**  I was knocked backwards.

**Robert**  We jumped backwards. Instinctively. Tremendously fast.

**John** Tremendously.

**Robert** To the extent where you could say there was no –
decision – no moment where we made a choice but
simply an entire nervous system's sudden and violent
response to threat. The brain was cut out of the process –
straight to the body – jump.

**John** Robert, we have been on this island which is forty
miles away from the nearest inhabited land which itself
is some forty miles away from a hospital if we could get
there given that the boat will not come for us till the end
of summer and we have no radio so we are utterly alone
and we have been on this island not more than an hour
and you have already smashed the door on top of me,
and blown us both up. You don't think, Robert, that it
might be wise – from now on – to at least try to think
before you act –

**Robert** You're cross.
    Which comes from fear – shock – fear – anger –
    I'm cross too. Now.
    Bloody hell.
    I nearly killed us.
    Christ.
    Now I'm angry – now – the adrenalin comes rushing –
heart beats and so forth – now – I'm sweating –

**John** I'll go and get the kit.

**Robert** Shaking – raging – fear comes after – which is
what it must be like for a soldier – under fire – because
we nearly died. Nearly.

**John** You bloody bugger, you bloody irresponsible
bugger.

*Ellen appears in the doorway.*

**Ellen** Hello.

**John** Excuse my French.

*Pause*

**Ellen** Soot-black on your faces.
Your hair, sir.
Like minstrels you look.
Like off of a film.

**Robert** It seems we were at the centre of a conflagration.

**Ellen** It would seem so.

**John** I'm afraid we haven't – tidied up much yet.

**Ellen** No.

**John** But we will, of course.

**Ellen** I came to ask if you'd be ready to eat soon?

**John** I'm certainly famished – you, Robert?

**Robert** Appetite – normal – it would appear – neither
hungry nor otherwise.

**John** Right. Right ho.
I think that means yes, Ellen.
I'll go and fetch the rest of the kit.
Clean yourself up, Robert.
And get the fire started – properly – would you?

*John exits.*

**Robert** Come in.

**Ellen** Thank you.
Stinks in here, sir.

**Robert** Birds – the fork-tailed petrel nests in burrows,
under stones. This place is half underground – it must be
riddled with them.

**Ellen** Uncle's caught a fowl for tea.

**Robert** Fowl?

**Ellen** A puffin.

**Robert** Never eaten a puffin.

**Ellen** Tastes of fish oil.

**Robert** Of course. It must. It must.
We taste of what we eat.
Humans, apparently, taste of sour milk and rotting flesh.

**Ellen** I'll see if I can get this fire going, sir.

*She starts to arrange and set the fire.*

Peat's dry enough, so it seems you need to put heather under it, sir, it's no use trying to start it without.

**Robert** Your hands.
They're . . .

**Ellen** Sorry, sir.

**Robert** What's wrong with them . . .?

**Ellen** Eczema, sir.

**Robert** Do you suffer from eczema?

**Ellen** Bad, sir. Since I was a bairn.

**Robert** Really?

**Ellen** It's nothing.
Makes my hands look like claws.
Put them in my pockets most of the time.

**Robert** Your hands don't look like claws.

**Ellen** Feel like claws. When they're looked at.
There's your fire.

**Robert** Thank you.

**Ellen** Well, sir.
I'll go and get tea.

**Robert** Wait.
  Shh.

**Ellen** What?

**Robert** Listen.

*Silence.*
  *Pause.*
  *A petrel calling from somewhere in the room.*
*An eerie, almost electronic sound.*
  *Robert listens intently.*

*Robert goes to investigate.*
  *In a corner of the chapel, amongst some debris,*
*there is a box.*
  *The noise is coming from the box.*
  *Robert looks into the box.*

An old candle box.
  She's made a nest in it.

*He shows Ellen.*

A fork-tail.
  Hen and chick.
  See how the she tries to bite me.
  Leach's fork-tailed petrel. *Oceanodroma leucorhoa.*
Somewhere between the size of a sparrow and a thrush,
slim and light, dark-feathered with a white rump and
the eponymous forked tail. It's webbed feet cold to the
touch. The hooked beak of the petrel family, black with
a soft tubular nostril. Dark, passive eyes. Beautiful –
don't you think?

**Ellen** It's a bird, sir.

**Robert** First time I've seen one.
  Here she is, in my own billet.
  They must be all over the island.

**Ellen** Is that what you've come all this way from London for, sir – that bird?

**Robert** Not only this one. We'll be surveying and taking photographs of all the birds. But, this is the real prize – Leach's petrel – barely known, never studied.

**Ellen** It must be a very special bird, for you to come all this way.

**Robert** There are rarer birds, but not many so hard to find. She lives at sea and only makes landfall to breed on outlying islands. The fork-tail's not rare, but where she nests, people are. Let's take her outside and see how she flies.

**Ellen** But that's her nest there, sir. With her baby.

**Robert** I want to see how she moves through the air.

**Ellen** Will she find her way back to her nest?

**Robert** I don't know.
   Let's find out.

   *Robert carries the box and bird outside.*
      *Ellen follows.*
      *Wind. Sea. Birds.*

Off you go.

   *The bird flaps away.*

**Ellen** She's going out to sea.

**Robert** Sickle wings, jerky, bobbing flight blown on the wind.

**Ellen** She'll tire surely. She doesn't glide like the gulls do.

**Robert** She'll stay at sea for two days, maybe longer, before she comes back to land.

**Ellen** Nest'll be cold now, sir. Chick'll die.

**Robert** Yes. Interesting, isn't it? Not very maternal of her.

**Ellen** I hope she finds her way home.

**Robert** When's food, Ellen? I'm hungry now.

**Ellen** Soon, sir. I'll fetch it shortly.

**Robert** Ellen, I notice you've taken to calling me 'sir'.

**Ellen** Uncle says I should, sir. Since you're from the ministry.

**Robert** Call me what you like.

**Ellen** Right, sir.

**Robert** My name is Robert.

**Ellen** Robert.

> *Ellen exits.*
> *Robert returns to the chapel. He replaces the nest box.*
> *John returns carrying kit, struggling.*

**John** Give me a hand with this stuff, will you?
That's the last of it.
Any sign of food?

**Robert** Apparently we dine on puffin tonight.

**John** For Christ's sake.
I thought we brought rations.

**Robert** Better to eat fresh.

**John** Puffin.
Puffin, though.
They're so endearing.

**Robert** They're also edible –
And . . .
Plentiful.

*The kit is all inside the chapel and heaved down onto the earth floor.*

**John** That's all the gear in. Looks in good shape.

**Robert** Is the camera safe?

**John** Let's have a look.

*He opens up a crate.*

Newspaper. I packed them in newspaper, you see.

**Robert** What about the flashes?

**John** All intact. Thirty-six.

**Robert** We'll survey the burrows first, find out where they all are. Take a few days to get the feel of the night-flighting. Then we'll take photographs. No point wasting flash.

**John** I'm bushed.
Arm hurts.
Up since half-six.
Famished.
Billeted in a mud cave half underground on a sodding rock somewhere in the middle of the sea.
We've only just got here and I want to go home.

**Robert** No you don't.

**John** I bloody do.

**Robert** Why do you say that?
What's the point in saying that?

**John** I'm just – moaning.
Letting off steam.

**Robert** We're here, Johnny. We made it. We're the first.

**John** I know.

**Robert** Nobody else has done this – nobody has come here, lived here and photographed these birds ever – we are the first.

This is your chance to experience the blinking limit . . .

**John** All right. At ease, sir. I'm only carping.

**Robert** Don't.

And don't 'sir' me.

**John** Sorry.

**Robert** You could be dead next year.

**John** I know.

**Robert** Sent off to some blinking foxhole and blinking gassed or something.

**John** Robert . . .

**Robert** So don't carp.

**John** I won't.

I'm just hungry.

. . .

Looking forward to a tasty puffin.

You got a smoke?

**Robert** Here.

**John** Ta.

> *Robert throws John a packet of fags.*
> *John lights up.*

Fag makes everything seem all right.

**Robert** I found a nest over there in the corner.

In an old candle box.

Fork-tail must have crawled in through a gap in the stonework.

**John** Let's have a look.

25

*John looks at the box.*

There's a chick.
    D'you think the mother will come back tonight?
    Maybe we've frightened her off?

**Robert** Humans don't scare her. She's a flyer. We lumber about so slowly. As far as she's concerned –
    We're just a larger variety of sheep.

*A blast of wind from outside.*

**John** Christ, we'll need to fix that door.
    The wind'll blow the fire out.

**Robert** The chapel, the bothy, the rest of the old village, it's all underground. Did you notice that?

**John** Give me a chance. I was humping kit.

**Robert** Burrows. We're living in a burrow.
    The fork-tails burrow.
    Nothing to stop the wind from one side of the Atlantic to the other and this rock in between – so the humans and the birds go underground.

**John** Very sensible.
    If we don't fix that door we'll freeze our balls off, excuse my French.

**Robert** The gannet takes a gamble, lays her egg on the cliff, spends nothing on the nest, there's eggs rolling about everywhere. Mess and madness. But the petrels invest – they dig – they come back. It takes a lot of effort to dig a pit.
    Gamblers and savers.

**John** What?

**Robert** Nature divides us into the gambler and the saver.
    I'm a gambler. You're a saver.

**John** Am I?

**Robert** You wrap things in newspaper.
Do you ever do the gee-gees?

**John** Do them?

**Robert** Bet.

**John** No.

**Robert** You'd hate it.
My family lost half of Hampshire because a paternal uncle of mine got into the gee-gees.
It's not an activity you ought to go in for.

**John** You do, though?

**Robert** I have done.
My point is this –
The cliffs and the burrows are related to each other.
Like men and women.

**John** Hold that, would you?

*Robert holds the door closed.*
*John hammers the nails in.*

**Robert** What d'you make of the girl?

**John** Ellen?
She's . . . nice.

**Robert** Sexually. What do you make of her?

**John** For Christ's sake, Robert.

**Robert** It's an important observation.

**John** It's damn prurient and none of your business as it happens.

**Robert** You exist in a stupor. Are you aware of that?

**John** I'm fixing a door. It's actually quite an energetic task.

**Robert** You are mentally stupefied.
The chloroform of the bourgeoisie.
Watch yourself.
Notice.
Rise out of the mess of the present and observe.
You are a sexually active male.

**John** I wish I were.

**Robert** You are – in terms of natural history.

**John** A hand on a pair of silk knickers at May Ball,
that's all the natural history I've ever experienced.

**Robert** Because you remain in a stupor.

**John** Just don't say that will you, Robert?
You do this – you perpetually insult.

**Robert** Why is it insulting?

**John** I'm trying to make this place watertight with no
help from you and all you seem capable of is a succession
of these somewhat stinging barbs about my sexual success.

**Robert** The comments sting because you are a sexually
active male who cloaks his natural urges in the stupefac-
tion of civilised morality.

. . .

She's got lovely jugs.

**John** What?

**Robert** Ellen.
Her jugs, good God, they're fabulous.

**John** I wouldn't know.

**Robert** On the ship, on the way over, she's leaning over
the side.
I caught a glimpse.

**John** That's it fixed.

28

**Robert** She's a young female of the species. It's fascinating to watch her so close up. She moves with an acute awareness of being watched and judged. Even the way she set the fire – before – when you were fetching the kit – every step she took was considered as to the eyes watching. And when she finished she stood back to be sure she'd be taken in – as a picture. Every movement of hers is arranged into a small performance for the spectator. When the performance is over she drops her eyes to the floor and awaits applause. She's concerned that her hands, which are riven with eczema, look like claws.
    They do, rather.

**John** I'll be frank with you, Robert. I don't think a chap ought to talk about girls like this.

**Robert** It's absolutely as it should be. She is sexually ready and on the look out for potential mates. We are both sexually ready. We observe her and she observes us.

**John** It's a damn fine line between that kind of talk and perversion.

**Robert** It will be interesting to see what happens.
    According to Darwin –
    We should both fight for her.

**John** I don't think that's wise.

**Robert** Don't worry. According to Darwin, she'll sleep with the loser as well. She's claimed by the winner but she'll mate with the loser when the winner isn't looking. That's her strategy.

**John** Look, old bean, I think I've made myself clear.
    If we're going to spend a month on this island with the girl and her clearly grim-faced uncle I don't want you talking about this type of stuff. It's asking for trouble.

**Robert** It'll be interesting to see.

**John** No it won't.
    We're here to survey the island. To take our notes.
    Write up our conclusions and send them in to the ministry. Girls – observation of – appreciation and general perverted staring at of their as you call them 'jugs' is not what we're here for.

**Robert** You're a prig.

**John** Perhaps.

**Robert** You can't be a prig and a scientist, you know.

**John** I can attempt to remain civilised in the face of –

**Robert** In the face of the truth. Turn your face to the truth, Johnny.
    The darkest thoughts, observe.
    Know thyself.

**John** That door is solid.
    Thank you, John, for fixing the door.
    Now I won't die of cold.

**Robert** Of course the interesting thing would be to observe the girl when she is not aware that she is being observed. That's the real meat of the work. To see that which is normally not seen.

**John** Will you stop this right now?

**Robert** How many girls have you had?

**John** Had?
    None – not that I care for your language on the matter.

**Robert** Your reticence interests me, that's all.

**John** I'm well aware of your conquests.

**Robert** There is no conquest.
    Only a surrendering to natural behaviours.

**John**  Yes, Robert, so you've told me, but do you enjoy it?

**Robert**  What?

**John**  Do you enjoy it? Fluffing some weeping lab assistant in her rooms on a Friday night?

**Robert**  I can't say I do or I don't.
It's interesting.
Are you referring to any specific incident?

**John**  Linda Jameson.

**Robert**  Oh her.

**John**  Did you enjoy it?
Did she have lovely jugs?

**Robert**  Not as lovely as Ellen's.

**John**  That's an opinion, not an observable fact.

**Robert**  On the contrary, old bean.
Ellen's breasts are perfect.
Two island hills.
Low and rounded.

**John**  Pale and soft.

**Robert**  You've noticed.

**John**  Of course I bloody have.
Excuse my French.

*Robert laughs.*
*Kirk enters.*

Mr Kirk.

**Kirk**  I see you've fixed the door.

**John**  Yes.

**Kirk**  I could have done that.

**John** I just thought –

**Kirk** It'll do.

*John finds a bottle of whisky amongst the gear.*

**John** Would you like some whisky, Mr Kirk, for our first night?
A welcome celebration.

**Kirk** I don't drink.
Doctor says it'll kill me.
I take pills –

**John** That's a shame.

**Kirk** Bloody doctor. He's on the mainland.
Go on, boy –
I'll take some.
It's never killed me yet.

**John** Sit down. It's only crates I'm afraid.

*John starts to pour whiskies.*

**Kirk** Ellen's bringing food across shortly.
You eaten fowl before?

**John** No.

**Kirk** I like my food in tins.
A tinned sausage.
You didn't bring any tins, did you?

**Robert** Just dry rations.
And whisky.

*The drams are poured in tin mugs.*

**John** Slainte.

*They drink.*

**Kirk** You don't look like ministry men.

**John**  Surveying's just leg-work. They send out the juniors.

**Kirk**  Counting birds.

**Robert**  The first comprehensive survey of the island's wildlife. We'll be taking observations. Studying the habits of the birds. The petrels in particular. This is an almost pristine habitat, Mr Kirk, it's barely been touched by humans. It's unspoiled.

**Kirk**  Preparations, is it? Hush-hush.

**John**  Preparations?

**Kirk**  For war.

**John**  There's nothing hush-hush about what we're doing.

**Kirk**  This island – all the way out here on the sea.
   This is a diamond for you ministry boys.
   Am I right?
   You can do what you like here and nobody need ever know.

**John**  It's more of a . . . an inventory – of the natural contents of the island.

**Kirk**  It'll soon be boats back and forth – and buildings for accommodation, and tins.
   I expect to be considerably inconvenienced.

**Robert**  The army may station a few troops. A gun maybe. But I don't think there'll be any interference with the annual.

**Kirk**  Don't mistake me, this island's sat here a hundred years waiting for its time. Sheep and fowl hardly make the trip worth taking every summer. If the island sheep can be put to use for military purposes let the military come. As long as I receive due compensation. I'm a patriot, but I'm not a fool.

**John** We're here to observe. That's all. We won't be in your way.

**Kirk** It's not yourselves – although you broke the door and who's to tell what else you'll break – but it's what you'll leave behind that I'll need compensated for.

**Robert** Our purpose is the close observation of nature, Mr Kirk.

**Kirk** God put the birds here for man to eat.
  And God, in all his graciousness, has afforded me the fowling rights.
  That's all I need to know about nature, boy.

*Ellen from outside.*

**Ellen** Bird's hot – can somebody open the door?

**John** Just a moment.

*John opens the door.*
    *Ellen enters carrying a metal pan.*
    *In the pan is a fried puffin and boiled kale.*

**John** It looks . . .

**Robert** It looks intriguing.

**Kirk** It'll do.
  Sit.

**John** It's only crates to sit on, Ellen. I do apologise.

**Ellen** Eat – while it's hot.
  There's boiled kale with it.

**John** Right-ho –

*Plates and forks are found in the kit.*
    *The food is set out.*
    *They begin eating.*
    *Wind from outside.*
    *Silence.*

**John**  Mmm.

**Ellen**  Is it all right for you?

**Robert**  It tastes like chicken cooked in axle-grease.

**Ellen**  I'm sorry, I –

**Robert**  Fascinating.

**John**  It's . . . nice.

**Kirk**  If you'd brought a tin.
You could have had a tin.

**Robert**  They should introduce it in restaurants.
As a delicacy – don't you think, John?
They'd lap it up in London.

**Kirk**  I've been to London.

**John**  Really?

**Kirk**  In the last war.

**John**  It must have been . . .

**Kirk**  It reminded me of nothing so much as a gannetry.

**John**  Right.

**Kirk**  A place of howling and squawking.

**John**  Yes.

**Kirk**  A place of random defecation.
Of eggs dropped and birds whirling.

**John**  I know exactly what you mean.

**Robert**  John's from Edinburgh, Mr Kirk.
Nobody defecates in Edinburgh. Do they, John?
Randomly or otherwise.

**Kirk**  Not yet. But it's coming.
Chaos and filth.

Women have begun to uncover their heads.
Cinemas have arisen.
We are becoming a pagan people.
Ellen and I are Christian still, thank God.

**John** I see.

*Kirk pours another whisky.*

**Kirk** Slainte.
A month's a long time for a study of birds.
They leave eggs.
What more do we need to know?

**Robert** Much much more, Mr Kirk.
There's always something waiting to be uncovered.
For example, did you know that in a gannetry about
a third of the eggs laid, don't belong to the male bird of
the pair guarding them?
They are bastards.

**Kirk** Is that a fact?

**Robert** Established fact.

**Kirk** The creatures know no better.
We are their husbandmen.
God made them for our food.

**Robert** A study I would like to undertake – using blood
type – would be to see how many children in London
belong to the male who guards them.
Or how many children in your village, for example?

**Kirk** The child I guard does not belong to me.
Not in the way you mean, boy.

**Ellen** Uncle – he was talking of birds.

**John** He didn't mean . . .

**Kirk** I guard her for a brother who lies at the bottom
of the sea.

**John** I'm sorry.

**Kirk** Drowned coming home from the war.

**John** How awful.

**Kirk** How does your natural history help you with that, boy?

**Robert** It's one of the most interesting questions of all.
  War.
  Is it natural?
  Two men fight, two birds fight, that's natural enough.
  But do you ever see a thousand or a million birds
flock together to attack a million others?
  Birds kill, but you never see them massacre.
  War and God.
  Perhaps they are peculiarly human inventions.

**Kirk** Godless are you?

**Robert** I only ask.

**Kirk** Shame.

**Robert** What do you think, Ellen?

**Ellen** I think it's a shame to serve you this poor fowl and make you eat it for your first time with us.

**Kirk** No shame in fowl, Ellen.

**Ellen** It is, uncle.
  We could have given them better food.

**Robert** We'll eat what you eat.

**Ellen** We may be remote from London, but we're not remote from the sensibilities of people such as yourself. We're not strangers to your world.

**Kirk** You're too familiar with certain sensibilities.

**Robert** Are you?

**Kirk** She is familiar with cinemas, and the darkness you find in them.

**Robert** Are you, Ellen?

**Ellen** You shouldn't be drinking, uncle.

**Kirk** I'm on the island.
    Away from the doctor.
    I'll do as I like.

**Ellen** You'll regret your speaking.

**John** Gosh – quite filling – puffin – isn't it?

**Kirk** The pagan is always desirous of something new.
    Desire being sown amongst us by the devil.
    It is his strongest weed.
    It chokes our soul.
    We should take what we're given and be thankful.
    But Ellen has given ground to desire.
    Ellen has visited the cinema.

**John** Do you like films?

**Ellen** I like some films.

**Robert** I like films.
    What films do you like?

**Ellen** I like a film – do you know a film called *Way Out West*?

**Robert** I do – I love that film –

**Ellen** I've watched that film thirty-seven times.
    How many times have you watched it?

**Robert** Once.

**Kirk** A hundred years ago there were people living on this island.
    Godless they had become through isolation.

Fallen to blasphemous practices.
Till God sent a famine that drove them to the mainland.
Now their descendants live amongst us and build
cinemas where there were churches before.

**Ellen** It is a bad thing, uncle.
We all agree.
Bad.
Wicked.
But we are on the island.
There is no cinema for me to visit here.
No need to speak of it.
If you're all finished.
I'll take the dishes to be washed.

**John** Let me help you.

**Ellen** It's all right – I can manage.

**John** Let me. Please.

**Kirk** Leave her.

**John** It's quicker with two hands.

**Kirk** I don't want to know what you do with your
hands, boy, in the presence of my niece.

**Robert** I think you can trust John, sir. John thinks girls
break if you touch them. He'll keep his hands to himself.

**Kirk** I'll carry the plates to the stream.

**Ellen** I can do the dishes fine myself.

**Kirk** This is my island, boy.
Decency will be observed upon it.

*Ellen and Kirk leave.*

**John** Bugger me, he's hard work.
Excuse my French.

**Robert**  Ask yourself this question, Johnny.
  To what military purpose can you put a sheep?

**John**  What?

**Robert**  When he was grilling us about the survey, he said that the ministry wanted the island for military purposes.

**John**  There's a war coming, everything's got a military purpose. He's just grubbing about for compensation.

**Robert**  He said the flock. He said the flock had a military purpose.

**John**  He's an old man.

**Robert**  Military purposes.

**John**  Perhaps he thinks the sheep are to feed the army.

**Robert**  He didn't say that.
  He implied there was a plan.

**John**  A top-secret sheep-related war plan?

**Robert**  I'm asking myself, why are we here?

**John**  To survey. Look, they'll be planning an artillery battery or something and . . . I don't know. The ministry probably don't know. There's a war coming and they want to seem like they're doing something.

**Robert**  I'm sitting in Cambridge. I get a call. Come and see the ministry, am I interested in going to the island? – of course I'm bloody interested – it's the chance of a bloody lifetime and I don't question it. I don't ask myself, why is the ministry interested in an an outlying island?

**John**  I suppose you could stuff explosives up a sheep's arse.
  A crack team of collies.
  Trained not to panic under shellfire.

Herding a flock of living sheep bombs behind enemy lines.
Come by, come by.

*He whistles for a sheepdog.*
*He makes the sound of an explosion.*

Achtung! Gottinhimmel!

*He makes the sound of an explosion.*

I don't think the ministry are interested in Mr Kirk's ewes, Robert.

**Robert** They're interested in something.

*Kirk re-enters.*

**Kirk** I washed the glasses.
Where's that whisky?

**Robert** Here.

**Kirk** Very civil of you.
Sit.

*Kirk pours the measures.*

Drink.

**Robert** To the ministry.

**Kirk** To the ministry.

**Robert** To a rewarding trip.

**Kirk** Rewarding. Aye.
Now tell me, birdman –
How many of my fowl are to die?

**Robert** This year?

**Kirk** Aye – how much am I looking at for the birds?

**John** I don't understand you, Mr Kirk?

**Kirk** The birds, boy, I've been told about the sheep but the birds – nobody's talked to me about the birds.

**John** That's what we're here for. To find out about the birds.

**Kirk** I need to calculate my losses.
In the letter they asked me to calculate my losses.

**Robert** What exactly did the letter say?

**Kirk** I cannot divulge its contents.
It was marked as a confidential communication.

**Robert** Of course.

**Kirk** I know the value of what's here now.
The question is, what am I to lose?

**Robert** Well, we would need to know what value the island holds for you.

**Kirk** It's grazing land. I hold the rights to the grazing. Eighty sheep. If I'm to lose my flock to this . . . thing, that's eighty sheep. And then, after. Will I be able to graze next year or will the land be poisoned? That's eighty times two which is one hundred and sixty sheep. But I'm not asking about the sheep . . . I'm aware of the destruction of the sheep. I'm asking about the birds.
And the birds – nobody has considered the birds.

**Robert** What have the ministry said to you?

**John** Robert . . .

**Kirk** They told me their plans.

**Robert** Of course.

**Kirk** But the ministry don't know about the fowling rights. They don't know that I take some two hundred fowl from this island every year. Does the germ kill birds? That's what I want to know.

**John** What germ? What are you talking about?

**Robert** They told you about the germ?
  I didn't realise the ministry had told Mr Kirk about the germ.

**Kirk** It was a slip of the tongue. Not my place to have mentioned it.

**John** What germ?

**Robert** John, it's that project.

**John** What project?

**Robert** The one they told us about.

**Kirk** Mum's the word.

**Robert** Exactly, Mr Kirk.
  Top secret.

**Kirk** That's the story.

**Robert** The letter must have been from Porton Down, was it?

**Kirk** That's right, aye.

**John** Porton Down?

**Robert** That's the project.
  Porton Down.

**Kirk** But what I want to know is – the birds – how many of the birds will I lose . . . how long? Because I need to make the calculation of my losses, d'you see? I need to make the calculation.

**Robert** Well, that all depends. It's difficult to say.

**Kirk** But you can guess.

**Robert** Well, which germ is it?

**Kirk** The man said it was the germ that causes
Woolsorters.
    There was a Harris man got it years ago.
    Black sores all over his arms, they said.

**Robert** Anthrax.

**Kirk** Is that its name?

**Robert** That's its name, Mr Kirk.

**Kirk** It's well named.
    It has the sound of the devil about it.

**John** Anthrax.
    Bugger me.
    Excuse my French.

**Kirk** I'll lose the flock to it. That's clear enough. But
they have asked me to calculate the losses per annum.
Now, the birds, the birds, you see – will they be lost, will
they be lost for a summer only? Because that is part of
the calculation.

**John** What on earth do the ministry want with anthrax?

**Robert** The ministry's intention, Mr Kirk, is to bomb
this island with anthrax in order to see how many living
things will be wiped out. And for how long.

**Kirk** Bombs. That'll not be good for the grazing.
    I'll want something for that.

**Robert** Mr Kirk, this island is a sanctuary.
    It's pristine. This cannot happen here. It must not be
spoiled.
    You'll simply have to recommend another.

**Kirk** I don't want to recommend another.
    I want to recommend this one.
    This one is mine.

**Robert** You don't seem to grasp – Mr Kirk.

If the ministry – if they infect it – the island will be dead – for years . . .

**Kirk** How many years?

**Robert** Nobody knows. Five, ten, twenty, fifty . . . It will not support life.

**Kirk** It is a useless lump of rock.

A pagan place.

I'd have sold it years ago if there was ever a buyer.

Let them have it for as many years as they need.

For seven hundred pounds my niece can be married and her husband given a share of a herring-drifter.

That is supporting life.

**Robert** No. No. No grazing here, no fowl taken – nothing.

**Kirk** It's a hard place to take a living from.

Let me be the last.

Let them compensate me.

**Robert** The island will die.

**Kirk** It has no soul.

And let that be the end of it.

Make your survey. Conduct your studies. Undertake your preparations.

We shall be the last people here.

To the ministry.

I must piss.

Tempted though I am to piss in the corner.

I will have a care for your comfort and take myself outside.

*Kirk exits.*

Bloody door's jammed.

*He laughs.*
   *He kicks it.*

It's broken again.

   *He laughs again.*

I'll want compensation for that door.

   *He exits.*

**Robert**  I should have realised.
Damn them.
Of course they were up to something.
The old man's face in Whitehall.
Over the desk when he asked me, in his eyes –
Deceit.
They don't want us to observe, Johnny,
They want us to take a census of the living dead.

**John**  We don't know that. We can't be certain.

**Robert**  The last wild scrap of rock and soil.
And they want to make a laboratory of it.
To enculturate it with their germ.

**John**  If there's going to be a war, we'll need weapons.

**Robert**  Let them use bayonets.

**John**  That's hardly sensible.

**Robert**  How dare they interfere!
What's the bloody point of coming here if it's to be
wiped out?

**John**  Maybe we can persuade the ministry.
If we make the scientific case –

**Robert**  The ministry doesn't care.
They have cities to destroy.
What does anyone care about an outlying island?

**John** Weapons have to be tested.
  Maybe we just have to accept . . . there are other islands
we can study.

**Robert** Let them infect themselves.
  This is a landfall.

**John** You have to admit Kirk has a point.
  It's a good choice. Remote and . . .

**Robert** He's nothing but a parasite.
  Did you see him?
  Sitting there gloating over the loot he's going to rake in.

**John** It's unpleasant but – perhaps . . .

**Robert** Perhaps nothing.
  Let them test their fucking bombs on London.

**John** Excuse your French.

**Robert** Why don't they infect the salons and gas the
slums?
  Spread botulism in the suburbs?

**John** Steady on.

**Robert** People are the problem, Johnny, not the birds.
  Wherever they gather they spread contagion.
  Let them take the mainland, and leave me the island.
  It's not his island.
  I've been here a day barely but it's more mine than his.

**John** He does have a claim to the place. His family hold
the lease.

**Robert** He's no more claim to this place than a tapeworm
has claim on the stomach it feeds off.

**John** We'll talk to him tomorrow.
  Maybe we can persuade him.
  He's drunk now – we'll wait till he's sober.

*Kirk re-enters.*

**Kirk**  That's better.
   One more drink.
   Then bed.

**Robert**  We were just talking, Mr Kirk, about how you are a parasite.

**John**  Robert . . .

**Robert**  I'm just making an observation.
   A parasite – or even a germ – who lives off a host body and then kills it.

**Kirk**  You watch your tongue, boy.

**Robert**  In the face of the annihilation of this . . . sanctuary, you're looking forward to fattening yourself up on the profit.

**John**  Robert –
   You could be a little more temperate.
   We all have to live together.

**Robert**  What right have you –?

**Kirk**  It is the ministry that is making the proposal.

**Robert**  Parasite.

**Kirk**  I take what I'm given and I'm thankful.

**Robert**  I won't allow it.

**Kirk**  It's not your place to allow or disallow, boy.

**Robert**  I have no 'place'.
   Don't 'place' me.

**Kirk**  You're a young Englishman who knows nothing.
   I thank God he gives me the forbearance to forgive you your tongue.
   Goodnight.

   *Kirk gets up to leave.*

**Robert** Mr Kirk.
  What's to stop me from hitting you?

**John** What?

**Kirk** Hold on, boy.

**Robert** I should hit him.
  It's obvious.

**John** Hit? Don't be ridiculous.

**Robert** Not hit, beat – beat.

**Kirk** Don't you lay a finger on me.
  This is my island.

**Robert** We're here. Forty miles from anywhere and
a month before we see another human.
  He's a weak old man.
  Let's knock some sense into him.
  Let's force him to write a letter to the ministry.
  Force him to sign.

**John** Don't be ridiculous.

**Kirk** I'm going to my bed.
  You boys have taken too much drink.

**Robert** Stay there.

*Robert holds the old man in front of him, his arms
pinned against his side.*

Hit him – you've done basic army training, haven't you?

**John** I will not hit him.

**Robert** Before the girl gets back.

**Kirk** I think it would be better if you take your hand off
my shoulder, boy.

**John** For God's sake, Robert.
  I'm terribly sorry about this, Mr Kirk –

**Robert** Beat him – if he doesn't change his mind, we'll beat him again.

**John** Apart from anything else it's against the law.

**Kirk** I will be informing the ministry about this.

**Robert** Be quiet, old man.
What's he going to do – call the police?
The man's drunk – he's an easy target.

**John** He'd call the police when we get back.
And if he didn't, I would.

**Robert** Would you?

**John** You hit him if you're so keen on hitting.

**Robert** What if we killed him?

**Kirk** You're deranged. Tell him to take his hand from me.

**Robert** Look, I'm just interested.
We're in a position to kill this man –
And no one would know.

**John** Ellen would know.

**Robert** He fell – he's drunk – he fell and hit his head – on the stone hearth.

**Kirk** ELLEN! ELLEN!

**Robert** Calm down.

*Robert puts his hand over Kirk's mouth.*

**Robert** There are some verifiable facts we have to consider here, John. If we don't stop him, this old man will sell the lease to the ministry and the island will die. Worse than that it will propagate death. It will become a killer itself.
The birds, John.

**John**  He's struggling.

**Robert**  Of course he's struggling. I've got my hand over his mouth.

**John**  Let him go.

**Robert**  Not until you have a better idea.

**John**  Persuade him – let's – Mr Kirk – we can be reasonable . . .

**Robert**  He can't answer you – my hands are over his mouth.

**John**  If it's money you're worried about, Mr Kirk, there is a possible income for you from tourism, Mr Kirk – have you considered that?

   *Kirk struggles, he's suffering.*

**Robert**  John – the man's point is valid. The ministry will give him the best price. If he wants to sell, he has every right. Tourism's a side issue – with a war coming there'll be no tourists anyway.

**John**  But there's a moral point. Mr Kirk – the island is a haven, it's unique, it's a wilderness – you surely don't want –

**Robert**  He's got to make a living, John.
   As long as he's alive.
   No. It really does come down to what he wants and what we want.

**John**  He's – Jesus, Robert – his eyes are rolling back he's –
   LET HIM GO.

   *Robert lets him go.*
   *Kirk breathes in heavily.*

51

**Kirk** Monstrous . . .
Monstrous . . .

**John** Sit down, Mr Kirk . . . please . . .

*John sits Kirk on a crate.*

**Kirk** Evil . . .

**John** You're all right now.

*Kirk groans.*

**Kirk** Ellen . . .

**John** I don't think he's well.
I think he's . . .

**Kirk** . . . bring Ellen . . .

**Robert** He looks like he's having a heart attack.

**John** Christ. Christ.

**Robert** He said he had pills.
He must have a weak heart.

**John** Where are your pills, Mr Kirk?

**Kirk** . . . Ellen . . .

**Robert** He's old. He's just old.

**John** Mr Kirk?
Do something.

**Robert** What?

**John** I don't know – water or – oh God.

*Kirk falls unconscious.*
*A moment.*
*His body fallen to the floor. Still.*

**Robert** He said himself he shouldn't have been drinking.

**John** Mr Kirk – Mr Kirk – wake up . . . wake up.
There's a first-aid kit. Get it from the bag will you . . .?

**Robert** I think he's beyond that.

**John** Mr Kirk –
Oh. Oh dear. Robert, he's . . .

**Robert** He's dead.

. . .

He's actually – he – expired.
Literally.
Taken his last breath.

**John** Mr Kirk.
Mr Kirk.

*John slaps Kirk.*

**Robert** I've never seen that before.

**John** What'll we tell Ellen? What'll we say to her?

**Robert** Nothing.
Not yet.
He looks like he's asleep.
Leave him there.
Let her make the discovery herself.

*Sudden sounds of thumping and bird calls from outside.*

**John** What the hell is that?

**Robert** Listen.
Listen . . .
The night-flighting.
The fork-tails.
They're coming in from the sea.

*Robert pulls open the door.*

Good God, it's chaos.
There are hundreds of them.

John, come and see.
They're throwing themselves at the ground.

*Ellen's voice in the distance.*

**Ellen** Birds have come, sir.

**Robert** The birds have come.

**Ellen** What a sight, sir.
Never seen it.

**Robert** Me neither.

**Ellen** Tumbling and falling.
Fighting.
Hundreds of them.
Falling out of the sky.
What a sight.
What a sight.


### THREE

*The sea crashing against rock.*
*The sound of thousands of seabirds.*

**Ellen** I sat with the body for three days and three nights
and on the morning of the third day I rose from a half-
dream and came out from the ground and into the
daylight. I walked to the good well looking for water
to wash and I saw the boy –
I see him at the cliff top standin' like he's got a
thought in his head a thought like a midge botherin' him
and he's looking away away out over the blackness of
the sea towards the mainland where we've come from
and I'm thinking why's he come here this boy this boy
to stand on this cliff and why's he come all the way here
from London from there where all waits for him why's
he come and as I'm thinking he vanishes over the cliff

edge like he's jumped and I so I howk up my skirts and go over to see where he's gone and I find the cliffs not sheer as it looks but sheep-pathed and he's running or more like falling down through the gannetry with the birds raising hell about him and stabbing for his head and the fulmars spitting oil at him and the noise and eggs falling and he's waving his hands about him and laughing and shrieking like he's found his own family and at last he reaches the water's edge where the sea swell's rising and falling and sucking and blowing at the rocks and I'm thinking he'll have trouble climbing back up here and I'm half away to fetch my uncle with his long rope for the fowling when I remember that uncle's dead and cold in the pagan chapel lying way way out of reach of me and so I stand and I remain watching and the boy starts to stripping his shirt and trousers from him his body white and skinny and he strips it all, he strips off all his clothes and they lie in the puddle of hot sun about him and I watch him and he doesn't know and he closes his eyes and his hands fall to touching himself to the giving of himself pleasure and there in the hot sun on the rock like a young gull preening I watch him and I'm thinking this is the thing of the most beauty I have ever seen this badness this fallen thought and I want to drink it this moment like a draught of whisky when the boy rises from the rock and all of a sudden dives into the sea and the boy swims the twenty yards it takes him to the stack of rock where he comes out and shakes himself down and he shivers the water from him and I think I think I think what is this feeling I'm having here this feeling of affection that's rising in me what is this feeling and I'm thinking this when all of a sudden he touches his hair and pulls it from his black gull eyes and he looks right at me and I realise –

This affection is an affection I have felt before.
This affection has come to me in my dreams before.

This is the same feeling, the way two sorrows can be the same the same affection as I have felt thirty-seven times in the darkness.

It is the affection I have felt for Stan Laurel.

Beautiful and tender, Stan Laurel.

And that is what I saw.

FOUR

*Afternoon.*
  *Inside the chapel.*
  *Ellen with the corpse of Kirk.*
  *She is shaving the corpse.*

**John** Ellen?

  *John enters. He is carrying a mug of tea.*

I brought you some tea.

**Ellen** Thank you.
  Sit.

  *She returns to her work.*

**John** You're shaving him.

**Ellen** He looked untidy.
  I washed his clothes.

**John** He looks a treat – tidy.

**Ellen** He looks old.
  He was old.
  With him these three nights.
  Watching him.
  Nothing makes you seem so old as to be dead.

**John** You haven't slept.

**Ellen** Nor have you.

**John** We've been working.

56

**Ellen**  Every night you've been out amongst the birds.
  And still bringing me tea.

**John**  We've slept in the day.

**Ellen**  You've been very kind to me.

**John**  Really it's – nothing.

**Ellen**  You see it in people. Goodness.
  A spirit.
  You can see it in them.

**John**  Maybe you should sleep.

**Ellen**  Maybe.

**John**  Ellen – I –
  Your uncle and you –
  Were you very close?

**Ellen**  My uncle was not a close man.

**John**  No.

**Ellen**  But he was not cold.

**John**  No.

**Ellen**  Most of the time I hated him.

**John**  I'm sure you didn't really.

**Ellen**  No – I did. For being an old man.

**John**  Yes well, all of us –

**Ellen**  I hated him.
  But it was a warm hate I felt for him –
  The hatred of a familiar thing –
  Your home, your village, the winter.
  It's gone.
  He was not cold.

**John**  The thing is, Ellen, the boat won't be coming for
another three weeks.

**Ellen** No.

**John** And unless some ship happens to pass there's no way of us leaving the island.

**Ellen** I've sat with him three days and three nights.

**John** So – he will – his body will . . . unless we –

**Ellen** I've done my duty.
It's enough.

**John** We really ought to bury him.

**Ellen** Yes.

**John** Is that all right?

**Ellen** We have to bury him.

**John** You don't mind?

**Ellen** He has to be buried.
It's all right.

**John** Good.
Well – not good, but . . .
Good.

**Ellen** Where's Robert?

**John** He's at the burrows. The fork-tails have all flown for the day. Every dawn we check the burrows to see which eggs have hatched and weigh the chicks to see how much they've eaten.

**Ellen** Have you weighed yourselves?
You've not eaten – I've cooked nothing for you.
You must be hungry.

**John** We've had our rations.

**Ellen** Nothing cooked.
I've neglected you.

**John**  No. I won't hear of it.

**Ellen**  You've slept in the bothy.
  While I've been here with the table and the fire.

**John**  Really, you mustn't think of it.

**Ellen**  He was old.
  We must bury him today.
  Before he begins to stink.

**John**  Robert and I have dug – in the cemetery – by the
others . . . well . . . a grave, I suppose.

**Ellen**  Is there weather?

**John**  It's a beautiful morning.
  Warm.
  And not even a wind.

**Ellen**  I'll sleep.
  And then we'll bury him.

**John**  Yes.
  We'll – I'll – I just – warmed up now . . .
  I only thought I'd bring you tea.

**Ellen**  Don't go yet.
  Would you sit with me?

**John**  Sit. Of course.
  Right-ho.

**Ellen**  I've been in and out of dreams.
  Don't know what I saw and what I dreamed.
  I seen you two boys out with your torches in the half-
dark.
  The flash lighting up your faces.
  And the birds flying all around you like a crowd of
women at fishmarket.
  I seen that – was that dream?

**John** We've been watching the fork-tails flighting these past two nights. We're going to take photographs tonight.

**Ellen** The noise they make.
  Thumping.
  Like the roof's come falling in.

**John** They're strange creaures. They live for two days at sea, and they make the most elegant flight, but when they come back to land, to their nests and chicks, they crash and thump on to the ground – they fly into each other – they attack each other. It's an amazing sight.

**Ellen** And you and Robert –
  Laughing and shouting.

**John** Did we disturb you?

**Ellen** When the torchbeams hit your faces you were smiling like children.

**John** He's always wanted to come to this island and study these birds. When we met at Cambridge Robert said, let's be the first to study them. I never thought we'd get the chance to come here.
  We don't mean to be disrespectful to your uncle.

**Ellen** Not a dream then – but it seemed like a dream.

**John** Not a dream.

**Ellen** I dreamed a bird.
  A gull sat in the hearth.
  Amongst the embers.
  Watching me.
  Black eyes on me.
  Seeing into me.

**John** That was probably a dream.

**Ellen** And I dreamed a boy swimming.

**John** Swimming.

**Ellen** Naked. In the sea.

**John** Could have been – a seal you saw.

**Ellen** He reminded me of Stan Laurel.

**John** Who?

**Ellen** Off of the films.

**John** Oh. I don't watch films I'm afraid.
Robert does. I read mostly.

**Ellen** I watched him lying on a rock in the sun.

**John** I haven't swum. Too cold. It must have been
Robert.
Robert swims. Didn't mention he'd seen you.

**Ellen** More likely a seal.
Or – maybe I dreamed it.
Does Robert have a girl?

**John** A –
Well, no. No.

**Ellen** Does he have his eye on someone in London?

**John** No. But –

**Ellen** Do you think he would notice me?
A girl of my type?
Does he –

**John** He has noticed you – he – said to me – the first
day, he said –

**Ellen** Did he? What did he say?

**John** He said you had – lovely eyes.

**Ellen** Did he?

**John** You do.

**Ellen** My uncle wanted me kept for a village man – a man at the fishing. Married and three-bairned, with my claws in a bucket of nets for the rest of my life. But uncle's dead now.
Isn't he?
So – I will cast my eye about whomsoever I like.

**John** Perhaps it's best if you – if we – eyes casting and so forth – if we don't – at least until the boat has come to take us back.

**Ellen** Yes.

**John** This is a very distressing time for you.

**Ellen** It's a strange time.

**John** When we're on the mainland.
You'll see things more clearly then.

**Ellen** You're kind.

**John** No.

**Ellen** A good friend to me for a stranger.

**John** You need to sleep.
Rest.

**Ellen** Thank you.

**John** That's it, lie there, that's it.
And I'll cover you with this blanket.
There.
And . . .
I'll stoke up the fire.
And . . .
. . .
Sweet dreams.

*John stokes up the fire.*
  *Ellen is asleep.*
  *Robert knocks on the door.*

**Robert** Blinking door's stuck again.

**John** Shh.
She's sleeping.
Hold on –

*Robert opens the door.*
*They speak in whispers.*

**Robert** Only half the chicks got fed last night.

**John** Keep your voice down.

**Robert** Only half – I weighed every one – only half had
an increase. Some nights some get fed, some nights some
don't – no discernible pattern. They all came back, but
some of them don't bring food.

**John** Why would they – what, deliberately? – starve
their chicks?

**Robert** It could be to do with the absorption of oil.
It takes time to metabolise oils, so perhaps if they're fed
too often they'd gain too much weight and be unable
to fly. But there is another possibility.

**John** What?

**Robert** That they're being tested.
How far can they go?
And if they fail –
The death of a weakling chick is a good thing.
A saving of resources.

**John** It seems unlikely.

**Robert** Does it?
Still – it's a promising start. Only here three days and
already we're breaking new ground.

**John** I can't help feeling that the survey, the island – it's
all been put into a little perspective by events.

**Robert** You're just tired.

**John** I don't know.
I'm in a daze.
Lost, a bit.

**Robert** We're a long way away from London.

**John** A long way from Edinburgh.
Three days here and I feel all I know's this patch of land in the middle of the sea and all the rest has faded away.

**Robert** It's a natural reaction.
We've witnessed one of the most – powerful moments it's given humans to observe.
We watched a man die.
Your response is natural –
Like when the paraffin exploded – in the moment you suddenly react and then – anger.

**John** It was our fault, Robert.

**Robert** A period of reflection when the chemicals, the adrenalin that's been swimming around in your system, suddenly dissipates and there's a slump.

**John** We could have done something.

**Robert** That's the slump.
Think about it – what could we have done differently?

**John** We shouldn't have given him whisky.

**Robert** He shouldn't have been drinking.

**John** No.

**Robert** And the strain of a day's sailing and then carrying those loads up the hill from the beach – it was obviously too much for him.

**John** He seemed at the top of his game –

**Robert** It's often the way –
   Look – he'd just had a full meal.
   His digestion was working overtime.
   He was drinking as well – which was putting a strain
on his heart.

**John** I suppose.

**Robert** And we challenged him. Challenged his authority.
   He stood up too quickly – the sudden movement must
have triggered something.

**John** He staggered, didn't he?

**Robert** The attack was probably already coming on.
   He seemed to have pain.

**John** He seemed – distracted.

**Robert** I held on to him.
   He looked like he was about to fall.

**John** I tried to get him to calm down.

**Robert** So did I – I had to physically hold him – because
he wanted to hit us.

**John** He – I mean although we argued with him – and
it did get quite heated – you didn't actually – I mean you
held on to him but you weren't actually exerting force –

**Robert** Good God, no – I didn't exert force.

**John** It was the kind of thing that a younger man would
easily have shrugged off –

**Robert** Exactly.

**John** I still feel as though we could have done something.

**Robert** Do you think so?
   I don't.
   It's strange, isn't it?

Look, Johnny, don't upset yourself.
It was my fault.
I challenged him.
I expected him to back down.
He should have backed down.
I've been cursing myself.
It was my fault.

**John** No. No, it was . . .

**Robert** If it was anybody's fault it was mine.

**John** It was an accident.

**Robert** If you say so.

**John** It was.

**Robert** But, you know, it was also a lucky accident.

**John** Lucky?

**Robert** Not for Kirk – obviously – but for the island.
For the birds.
The ministry will never get their hands on the island
now.
With Kirk gone –
They're waiting for a letter that will never come.
They'll forget about it.
They've probably forgotten already.
We can do what we like, John.
Complete a full study of the fork-tail.
An absolute first.
Not just the fork-tail but the whole island.
A whole, pristine, unobserved, unsullied, pure
environment.
Only for us.

**John** They'll want to see our report, though. We have to
do a report.

**Robert** We lost it.

In the files.

We'll deposit a copy somewhere in some departmental basement under 'P for Petrel, habits of' . . .

It'll never be found.

**John** It all seems a bit . . . rash . . .

**Robert** Who's to stop us?

**John** Nobody, I suppose.

**Robert** No one will notice. Not for months and by then they'll have contaminated some chunk of Dartmoor with their poison.

**John** What about Ellen?

**Robert** What about her?

**John** She holds the lease on the island now. It's hers.

What if she wants to sell it?

**Robert** Ellen won't be a problem.

**John** We can ask her not to. Persuade her.

**Robert** We can do what we like.

That's the luck of it.

When the old man died – it was like a fog fell away – I realised nobody really knows we're here.

We can do as we please.

We're alone.

Dead to the world and –

Free.

Look at him.

Lain there – he bears the shape of a living thing but every thing about him is still and dead. A stone. And then you see her sleeping, tiny tremors of movement passing across her skin – her eyes, her finger, the breast rising and falling, a shift of bodyweight.

She's at rest, but she's a living thing.

**John** She's beautiful.

**Robert** He's beautiful too. His is the beauty of absence.
The way an outlying island is more beautiful than the
mainland. Things at a distance are always more
attractive – a girl, a hill.
  Looking at him you see life, at a distance, receding.
  Looking at her, and looking at him, you realise that
when people say the dead look as if they're asleep – they
are either not looking closely enough at death, or they
are not looking closely enough at sleep.

**John** He's beginning to smell.
  I noticed.

**Robert** Maybe we should bury him now.
  Before she wakes up.

**John** Don't you think she might want to say goodbye?

**Robert** He's dead.

**John** I know but – the final moment – the last time she
sees him.

**Robert** She doesn't want to see him humped about like a
sack of potatoes.

**John** I suppose not.

**Robert** The pit's dug.
  We'll put him in it.
  And then we'll wake her.
  Cover him.
  A few words in my capacity as senior chap.
  And then it's over.

**John** Come on then, give us a hand, you take his feet.

**Robert** Got him.

**John** Right-ho. Lift.

*They lift.*

**Robert** He's a heavy beggar.

**John** To me, to me . . .

**Robert** Shh. You'll wake her up.
Get the door.

**John** It's stuck.

**Robert** Give it a tug.

**John** I'm about to drop him.

**Robert** Hold on, swing him round – I'll have a try.
Watch the tea.

*They knock the mug of tea over.*
*It clatters.*

Watch where you're going.

**John** I can't hold on to him much longer.

**Robert** Here we go.

*He tugs the door.*

Come on . . . come on . . . it's jammed –

*It comes free.*

**John** Watch out.

*John falls, knocks Robert, the body falls.*
*Ellen wakes up.*

**Robert** Oww.

**John** Shh.

**Ellen** What are you doing?

**Robert** Bloody idiot.

*He cuffs John.*

**John** Oww.

**Robert** Now look what you got us into.

*Ellen laughs.*
*The boys scramble to retrieve the situation.*

**John** Ellen, I'm most terribly sorry.

**Robert** We wanted to lay him out before you woke up –

**John** Please – we'll – I'm so sorry about this.

**Ellen** That's another fine mess you got me into.

*She laughs again.*

**John** What?

**Robert** I see.
I suppose it is a bit –
Comical.

**John** It's not funny at all.

**Robert** Laurel and Hardy – she's talking about –

*Ellen whistles the tune.*
*Ellen laughs again.*

**John** I think it's rather morbid.

**Ellen** Hit him again.

**Robert** Why you . . .

*He cuffs John again.*

**John** Oww.

*Ellen laughs.*

**John** Is this part of the joke?

**Ellen** You boys.
  You're a tonic.

**Robert** Stanley . . .

  *Robert cuffs John again.*

**John** Oww.

  *Ellen and Robert are in hysterics.*

**John** I really can't see the joke.

**Robert** No.

**John** We simply fell over.

**Robert** I know.

**Ellen** Hit him again.

  *Robert cuffs John.*

**John** Oww.

  *John cuffs Robert back.*

**Robert** Owww.

  *Ellen is practically wetting herself.*

**John** I just don't see where the humour is.
  The whole thing's quite unpleasant.

  *John stands up.*

I don't know about anyone else but I need a stiff drink.

**Robert** Do you, John?

**Ellen** A stiff drink?

  *They collapse again.*

**John** What's so funny about that?

**Robert** (*doing an impression of Kirk*)
  You need a stiff drink.
  What about me?

**John** Oh for God's sake.
It's a corpse, Robert – not a ventriloquist's dummy.

**Robert** I'm sorry.

**Ellen** He's dead.
He doesn't care.
And I'm . . .
Awake.
Half-dreaming for three days.
And it's enough.
Seeing him dead there.
It's the first time I've known that I'm alive.
I want to drink.
I've never drunk.
I want to drink.

**John** It's awfully early in the morning for it.

**Robert** No, she's right.
Why not drink?
Here – we'll all have some.
We work at night, we sleep in the day, we can do as
we please.
Isn't that right, Ellen?

*He pours her a drink.*
*Ellen coughs.*
*Drinks more.*

**Ellen** That's right.

**John** I'll have one.

**Robert** Me too.

*They all drink.*

**Ellen** Happy.
Do you think it's normal to be happy at death?
Maybe I'm a monster.

**Robert** Why shouldn't you be happy?

**Ellen** I'm supposed to weep.
  He's blood of mine.

**John** I've never been bereaved. I don't know – can't
know –

**Robert** Nature does not require that you weep for the old.
  Birds on the cliff top clear the corpses without pity.
  Your feelings are perfectly natural.

**Ellen** Awake. Is all. After winter, spring.

**Robert** Here – in a natural environment – death means
exactly what it should. More room for the young.

**Ellen** Like when the lights go down in the cinema.
  And the music starts.
  And the film begins.
  Only now I'm in it.
  With you two.

**Robert** Laurel and Hardy.

**Ellen** Laurel and Laurel.
  You – your hair sticky-uppy from being under your hat.
  Your eyes black and –
  And Johnny – always anxious and lost-looking.
  Laurel and Laurel you are.

**John** I wish I knew what you two were talking about.

**Ellen** I've had three nights in a half-dream.
  I've felt alone.
  I don't want you to go back to the bothy.
  It's cold in the bothy.
  This is to be my island now and you my guests upon it.
  I want you to stay here.

**John** I'm not sure that's . . . for the best . . . is it?

**Robert** It makes sense for us to share the same room.
For heat.

**John** But there's still weeks till the boat comes.

**Ellen** Let there be weeks.
We have food.

**John** You don't mind . . .?

**Ellen** They call this the chapel but it is a pagan place.
This was their church, you know, if church they
called it.
Their priest lived here.
They were fallen, the last people, uncle wouldn't have
us talk about them but in the village they spoke of it.
Fallen. They'd come to the mainland from time to time
and take a girl out to be married and the people would
give them a fallen girl – never a girl like me – because
the fallen were damned already and only fit to be brides
for pagans. They'd speak of it as a warning but I used to
dream of the boat coming to take me. Wouldn't you?

**John** Well I don't know, I –

**Robert** Of course.

**Ellen** Do you know how the island came about – truly?

**John** Volcanos.
There's a fault line under the Atlantic –

**Ellen** Truly.
At the beginning of time there was a giantess, and she
was in the business of carrying rocks from Ireland over
to Scotland where she was building a home for herself
and her daughter. So every morning as the sun rose she
filled her basket with stones and hitched up her skirts
and walked out from the beach into the sea – which for
her was no more that a burn for the crossing. And so it
was that from time to time as she delivered her loads she

74

slipped sometimes on the ocean bottom and spilled her stones – and the stones that fell were made islands and that was how we came to get Lewis and Harris and Skye and Mull and Rum and Muck and Eigg and so it was also that the pebbles she dropped from her basket fell and made islands also and that is how we got the islands outlying – the flannans and the monachs and the shiant and all the islands outlying the outliers, the black islands and the sheep islands and the goat islands and the small islands and all those of that desert type that lie scattered in the sea. And so it was that one day the giantess was hungry and she saw a bird she wanted the eating of flying far out in the distance so she bent reached her hand into her basket she was carrying and she fetched a stone which she threw at the bird with all her strength to bring it down. But the stone missed its target and sailed on and on to the north far out forty miles or so before it hit the cold sea and settled down on the sea bottom and it was a mile broad and a half-mile long and that was this island, the most outlying of all the islands and the one which has on it the chapel of the priest who was fallen and driven out from the mainland with his woman and who came here to hide himself away and there were his people here who lived for three hundred years until they were cleared by a famine from God and they came to the mainland once more and were saved. And the island was kept for sheep only and shepherds and the houses to fall to ruin.

And that is the true history of this island.

This island which is mine.

**John** What will you do with it . . . after you go back?

**Ellen** I don't know.

It has no use.

Maybe build a house on it and use my claws at the fowling and grow kale to live.

Maybe sell it and build a cinema.

75

**Robert** You can do exactly as you please.

**Ellen** Drink.
    Let's bury him.
    But first – we must have a service.

**Robert** Yes. A funeral. He must have a send-off.

**Ellen** A few words.

**John** Robert said he was willing to say a few words . . .

**Ellen** He must have a eulogy.
    I'll speak it.
    Sit – the congregation must sit.

*The boys sit.*

**Ellen** Now you must look like stones.
    Still and in heavy consideration of God.
    That's right.
    So.
    We are gathered here to pay tribute to Iain Kirk.
    An island man.
    He was a man – look at him – dead there – up in
heaven now –
    He was a man –
    Who knew the evils of womanhood.
    Who fought all his life against the decoration of nails.
    Who kept our house shut against the cinema.
    Who saw Stornoway for what it was – a house of sin.
    Who was never happier than when amongst fish –
    Or at the funeral of an old friend.
    Who knew well the value of pennies.
    And oatmeal.
    And darkness.
    And work.
    And now he is gone.

**Robert** Amen.

**John** I don't know if that's appropriate.

**Ellen** Amen.
A hymn. A hymn now.

**John** I'm afraid I only know episcopalian hymns.

**Ellen** This is a pagan place.
We'll sing a pagan hymn.
After me.

'In the Blue Ridge mountains of Virginia,
On the trail of the lonesome pine.
In the pale moonshine, our hearts entwine
Where she carved her name
And I carved mine.
Oh June,
Like the mountains I'm blue.
Like the pine,
I am lonesome for you.
In the Blue Ridge mountains of Virginia,
On the trail of the lonesome pine.'

*John and Robert join in.*
*Eventually lustily.*
*The song ends.*

**Ellen** Now put him in the ground and cover him.
He's gone from here.

### FIVE

*A phosphorescent flash.*

*The early hours of the morning, towards the end of the night-flighting.*
*Darkness outside.*
*Heavy rain and wind.*

*Robert and John are outside the chapel taking night photographs of the birds arriving at their burrows.*

**Robert** Did you get it?

**John** I don't know. I can't see a bloody thing.

**Robert** Me neither. Only three left.

**John** Jesus! Blinking sod!

**Robert** What?

**John** Bloody gannet got me in the leg.

**Robert** Come on.

> *Inside the chapel, Ellen is sitting by the dying embers of the fire, in lamplight; she has opened Robert's notebook and is reading from it.*
> *From the candle box, the cheep of the fork-tail chick.*

**Ellen** 'Day Four. New Moon. Thirty-two birds returned to their burrows. Fifteen burrows left unattended. See map below. Two eggs remain unhatched, 21 and 44. Two adults lost in predation by gulls.'

> *A second phosphorescent flash.*

**John** I can't feel my fingers.
I'm numb.

**Robert** Did you get her?

**John** Perfect.

**Robert** Last one. Wall by the field.
Come on.
Soon be done.

**John** I'm soaked to the buggering bones.
My actual bones are wet.
I'm going to die.

**Robert** You can't die yet.
I haven't given you permission.

**Ellen** 'Nest Number One, chick remains unattended since the first day.'

That's you he means.
Number One is you.
Because he found you first.

*Ellen goes over to the candle box.*

Poor chick.
All the mother birds come home but yours.
Who's to keep you?
Who's to give you warmth?
Poor chick.

*A phosphorescent flash.*

**Robert** Beautiful.
Did you see?

**John** I saw.

**Robert** Perfect.

**Ellen** He's a bad man.
Isn't he a bad bad man?
A bad bad man he is.

*Ellen takes a small stone from the floor of the chapel.*
*She puts the stone in the hearth.*
*She finds a piece of oily rag beside the lamp.*
*She lifts the stone from the fire and wraps it up in the oily rag.*
*She puts the wrapped stone in the candle box.*

Keep you warm a while.
Fires dying.
Need more peat.

*A moment.*
*The boys outside the door.*

**John** I can't open it.

*They enter.*

**John** (*imitating Kirk*)
'I'll want compensation for that door.'

*Robert and John giggle.*
  *Slightly hysterical.*

**John** 'If you boys weren't come here to my island.'

**Robert** 'Making your studies of jugs.'

**John** 'Interfering with my sheep.'

**Robert** 'Falling to blasphemous practices.'

**John** 'It would be a door serving its purpose.'

*Ellen pulls her shawl over her head.*
  *She opens the door.*
  *Ellen leaves into the darkness and rain.*

*The boys are soaked, cold, muddy and exhausted.*
  *They sit. Silent.*
  *John, scrabbles about in his pack.*
  *He finds a packet of biscuits.*
  *He eats one.*
  *He throws one over to Robert.*
  *Robert catches it.*
  *Robert eats the biscuit.*
  *John takes his boots off.*
  *Takes his socks off.*
  *Squeezes the water out of them onto the floor.*

**Robert** You are my madeleine, Johnny, do you know that?

**John** What?

**Robert** They say that smell is the key to the door of memory, don't they? Didn't old Proust get transported to the bosom of his mother by a whiff of cake?

**John** Buggered if I know.

**Robert** He did, no, he did and I must say . . . catching the aroma of your socks, Johnny, wafting across the chapel like some . . . like some pagan incense . . . a heady mix of regurgitated fish oil and sweaty wool, I am transported . . . I really am.

**John** Are you, old bean?

**Robert** I am.

**John** And where are you transported to?

**Robert** Somewhere in between Linda Jameson's thighs.
   Of course, that's not a place you would be familiar with.
   Is it?

**John** Transported, are you?
   You asked for it.

*John takes his sock and rubs it in Robert's face.*

**Robert** Get off.
   Get off.

**John** Not until you apologise.

**Robert** Never.

**John** You know you can't win.

**Robert** I submit.
   I'm sorry.
   Mercy.

*John breaks off.*
   *Sits back down.*
   *Sniffs his sock.*

*Robert laughs. John laughs.*

We did it.
All the burrows photographed.
We got flying, fighting, feeding, everything.

**John** We're the first.

**Robert** The first by a mile.

**John** We'll die if we don't get dry.

*John starts to take off his wet clothes down to his underpants. He hangs his clothes off the table.*

Where did Ellen go?

**Robert** She's probably gone to get breakfast.

**John** I'm starving.

*Robert also strips and hangs his clothes.*
*He pulls a blanket over his shoulders.*
*He takes a damp notebook from a pocket of his trousers and sits down to write up his notes.*

**Robert** What time is it?

**John** I don't know.
Nearly dawn I suppose.
I don't even know what day it is.

**Robert** Most of the chicks are hatched. Only a few weeks and they'll be flying. They'll start going south.

**John** I don't blame them.
If this is what it's like in midsummer.
How people ever survived a winter in this place is beyond me.

**Robert** You adapt. That's all. You stay underground.

*John goes to the candle box.*

**John** This one's still not been visited.
Old Number One.
He's still alive.

**Robert** I know.
I don't understand.
Four whole days without warmth.
He should be dead.

**John** Why doesn't his mother come back?

**Robert** I don't know.

**John** Maybe she died at sea.

*John gets a cigarette.*

Poor little bugger.
You look out at sea and there's so much of it.
And it all seems so buggering empty.
You got a light.

*Robert throws him a lighter.*
*John lights up.*

**Robert** We have to follow them.

**John** What?

**Robert** They live at sea. We're only getting glimpses of them here.

**John** I suppose.

**Robert** They'll all be flying soon. What if we tag them, before they leave, every one, adult and chick . . .?
What if we follow the migration? All the way down to the Azores.

**John** That would be . . . it would – has anybody ever done that?

**Robert** No.

**John** To follow an entire colony.

**Robert**  Observe the pairing patterns. The survival rates. Study the distances travelled at sea. Follow them south and then all the way back here again – next summer.

And this is only one population.

There are colonies in Greenland, Newfoundland . . . in the Pacific even.

Imagine it. Imagine really understanding them, John.

**John**  The ministry won't send us to Greenland.

**Robert**  We don't need the ministry. We can do it ourselves.

**John**  Hardly.

**Robert**  Why not?

**John**  A chap has to earn a living.
Not much money in birds.

**Robert**  Sod money.
Money's never a problem.
We don't need much anyway.
Some grub, we've got kit.
It's not as if there's anything to spend it on.

**John**  What if there's a war?

**Robert**  There won't be.

**John**  D'you think?

**Robert**  Look, fuck their war.

**John**  Steady on.

**Robert**  Let them. Let them tear each other to pieces. Good.

The more of them that die the better.

We'll get out of it. Anybody with half a brain can get out of a war. It's only the boneheaded, the cattle, the boys who like sport who walk out in front of guns.

They bloody love it. Let them. We'll be far away.

**John** I was thinking of applying for the air force.

**Robert** Why in Christ's name would you want to do a stupid thing like that, Johnny?

**John** I don't know.
I suppose I fancied being a flyer.

**Robert** Then follow the birds.
You want to come back, don't you?
You do want to?
You want to come back for Ellen.

**John** Of course I do.

**Robert** I don't know why you flinch.

**John** No, I don't imagine you do.

**Robert** You draw back.

**John** I don't know what you're talking about.

**Robert** Your hand hovers, Johnny, it's quite transparent . . .
A half an inch from her skin when she stands by you.
And then you draw back.

**John** I do not.

**Robert** You must sicken,
With every dawn that passes and yet still she remains untouched.

**John** Don't, Robert.

**Robert** Don't what?

**John** You know perfectly well what I'm talking about.

**Robert** You'll tire.
Hovering is tiring.
Eventually you'll lose strength.
Your hand will move.
You'll fall.
It's perfectly natural.

**John** How do you do it, Robert?
You always – you . . . get what you want.

**Robert** Do I?

**John** That's what it seems like.
To us ordinary mortals.

**Robert** How could you possibly know what I want?
You don't even know what you want, John.

**John** I want to remember what it feels like to be warm.
I want to sleep.

*John gets up. Goes through his kit. Finds a pair of
shorts and a vest. He takes off his underpants and
puts the shorts and vest on.*

**John** We may be far away.
But there is a boat coming.
At the end of the summer.

*Ellen returns.*
   *She stands in the open doorway.*
   *She sees John changing.*

**Robert** How do they fly?
You saw them in the storm.
How do they do it?

**John** I could hardly open my eyes.

**Robert** There was a moment, in the dark, crossing the
bog near the cliff top, when the mist was everywhere and
the rain was whipping in off the sea and I thought . . .
My clothes are wet. My skin is wet.

**John** I was too numb to think.
Except bacon and eggs.
I kept seeing bacon and eggs and a hot fire.
Hovering in front of me.
Just out of reach.

**Robert** The whole world's water . . . the world's water . . .
Nine-tenths of our bodies is made of water. The substance
of us is water. I thought . . . so little of us is solid we
might as well be made of mist. Mist clinging to hollow
bones.

*Outside the chapel, the call of a petrel.*
    *Ellen still waits.*

**John** They must be dry by now.

*Ellen enters.*

**Ellen** Never dry in front of a fire like that.
Fire's about dead.
You'd have let it go out.

**John** Dry enough. They'll dry on. Once the fire's going.

*John puts his clothes on.*
    *Ellen puts peat on the fire.*

**Ellen** There's a bird outside.
The rest have settled but there's one still flying above
the chapel.
She's calling fit to burst.

**Robert** The light! It's the light!
You blinking idiot.
That's his mother.

**John** Whose mother?

**Robert** Number One.

**Ellen** She's calling and calling.

**Robert** She won't come because of the light.

**John** Come in – in here?

**Robert** They always land at night, why?

**John**  To avoid predation.

**Robert**  To avoid the gannets who'd snap them out of the sky like that.
    So they wait for dark to come back to their nests.
    Dark – dark – she doesn't know what's sun and what's lamp.
    Dark's all she wants.
    No wonder she's left the chick five days.
    She's been waiting for night to fall and it never has.
    Switch the lamp off.

*Ellen blows the lamp out.*
    *The chapel is dark but for the glow of embers from the fire.*
    *Robert crouches in front of the fire, the blanket round his shoulders.*

**Robert**  Get the camera.

**John**  I can't see anything.

**Robert**  Quiet.
    She'll come in if we're quiet.

*They are all quiet.*
    *John looks for the camera in the dark.*
    *John knocks into the table.*

**John**  Owww.

**Robert**  Shut up.

**John**  Sorry.
    Found it.
    Nearly broke my shin.

**Robert**  Will you shut up, you blinking idiot.
    Stand by the candle box.

**John**  Will you not call me a blinking idiot.

*Ellen giggles.*

**Robert** I hear her.
She's coming.
Ready.

*In the darkness.*
*The flapping of a bird as it enters the chapel.*
*The bird makes her way swiftly to the nest.*
*The bird calls.*
*The chick calls.*

*A phosphorescent flash.*
*In the flash, Robert, crouched in the hearth, blanket*
*around his shoulders – a bird.*
*Ellen looking at him.*

*Darkness.*


SIX

*Night.*
*Weather.*
*A real storm.*
*Ellen and John in the chapel.*
*John is processing negatives.*

**Ellen** He's still out there.
It's darkening.
Rain's come heavy.

**John** He shouldn't be out tonight, he'll freeze, but he
insisted on it. He wanted to watch them flying in a
storm.

*He puts the plate into the processing canister.*

**Ellen** Abracadabra.

**John** What?

**Ellen** What magic you got hidden in there?

**John** It's not magic.

**Ellen** Magic to me. Pictures coming out of water.

**John** It's the chemical process. The light reacts with the film to make a plate. The plate reacts with the fluid to make a negative. Once the negative is fixed, you wash it. And then you get the image.

*He pours out the first fluid and pours in the second.*

**Ellen** Light. Water. Magic.

*She retrieves a processed negative.*

**John** A fork-tail chick.
A week old.
This one hatched on the second night.

**Ellen** It's a picture of Robert.

**John** It's a fork-tail chick.

**Ellen** It's Robert.

**John** Robert's in the picture.
He's holding the chick.
A human figure helps to visualise the scale.

**Ellen** The chick fits in the palm of his hand.
His eyes.
Look at them.
Do you see it?
What he does with his eyes. When he looks at a person.
When did you meet him?

**John** At college. We were both interested in natural history. He – I met him – I don't remember the exact moment. We sort of fell in together.

**Ellen** He picks you out.

**John** He's mostly, generally speaking, a trial.
   Quite liable to leave halfway through dinner, or to talk about the sexual habits of primates to a roomful of dowagers.

**Ellen** He's always looking about.

**John** What I can say for Robert is that he has some gift for observing nature. Better than anyone I've ever met. In so far as one can predict these things I suspect he may be very great in the field and –

**Ellen** Very great.

**John** So one holds on to his coat tails given the chance and puts up with the sheer bloody irresponsibility of the man.
   Excuse my French.
   He shouldn't be out there.
   The lightning.
   Maybe I should go and get him.

**Ellen** He watches me.

**John** I know. I know.
   He does the same to me.

**Ellen** As though I'm worth watching.

**John** You learn to ignore it.

**Ellen** I know what he wants.

**John** He doesn't want anything.

**Ellen** He does.
   Five days he's been watching me.
   This morning I woke up.
   I opened my eyes.
   And he was sitting by the last embers.
   His eyes on me like hands.
   Touching.

**John** If you felt uncomfortable – because I can – talk to him if you want.

**Ellen** I didn't feel uncomfortable.

**John** Oh.
Well. I . . . I see.
If –
Maybe I should get him.
The lightning.
It's really quite –

**Ellen** I rose, he watched me rising, the morning was warm.
I went to bathe.
At the stream.
I looked up the hill towards the village.
And he was still watching.

**John** When you were bathing?
Good God.

**Ellen** I wondered if he would come to me but he stayed where he was.
I think he's afraid of me.

**John** Now see – Ellen, if you have feelings for Robert,
And I don't pretend that I can deny he's spoken to me about –
That he has reciprocal –
But only in the sense that –
Any man would.

**Ellen** Any man?
Claw-handed?

**John** I – your hands are –
I didn't notice – I wouldn't say they were –
What I mean is any man – essentially alone with a woman of your – is bound to feel –

**Ellen**  What about you?

**John**  Well I – of course – but only in so far as – it's . . .

**Ellen**  As far as what?

**John**  It's natural, that I should feel . . .

**Ellen**  Natural.
But you will not name it.

**John**  What I want to say is that Robert – he's . . .
A –
The way he wants you is –
Purely . . .
Not genuine affection.
So I think you should be careful.

**Ellen**  Abracadabra.

*John removes the processed negative from the canister and places it in the bath for washing.*

**John**  He is not a man who will marry.
Or at least, if he does, I don't believe he'll make
a woman happy.

*Ellen laughs.*

**Ellen**  You're like uncle.
Marrying me off.
I said nothing about marriage.

*Ellen looks at the new picture. Ellen laughs.*

I don't see what's so funny.
It's not bloody funny. Excuse my French.

**Ellen**  This picture – this is not a bird.

**John**  What?

**Ellen**  This one here – no bird in this picture.

**John**  No – it's – Robert must've – oh, my God.

**Ellen**  That's a picture of me.

**John**  I had no idea – this is – scandalous . . .

**Ellen**  It's me.
Never seen a picture of me before.

**John**  He had no right.
No right at all.

**Ellen**  At the stream. In the morning.
My body.

**John**  You were bathing.
. . .
He –
I'll –
I'll put it on the fire.
Don't worry. I've not looked at it. I've – nobody will
see it.

**Ellen**  Am I so monstrous you'd rather it burned than
look at it?
. . .
Give it to me.
Hang the picture up.
Let it dry.

**John**  You want to keep it?

**Ellen**  I've never seen myself.
Look at it.

**John**  You look . . .
And it certainly doesn't take away from the sheer
liberty of taking the picture – but you do look –
Very beautiful.
If you don't mind me saying so.

94

**Ellen**  I don't mind.

**John**  I'll have a word with him.
I'll get him –

**Ellen**  Don't.
Let him be.
Look at the picture he's made of me.
This is how he sees me.

**John**  No –

**Ellen**  Yes –

**John**  It's – I'm warning you – it's instinct.
Animal –

**Ellen**  Natural.

**John**  You can't.

**Ellen**  I can.
This is my island.
Nobody here, except Robert, and me and you.

**John**  Simply because we are somewhat isolated –
There are limits of decency which we must observe.

**Ellen**  I've upset you.

**John**  He has upset me.

**Ellen**  I have broken the limits of decency.

**John**  No – but . . .

**Ellen**  I will break them again.

**John**  Have him then.
You have him.

**Ellen**  Why are you angry?

**John** I'm going to get him.
　 I'm going out.

　 *He tries to open the door.*
　 　 *It sticks.*

Bloody door.

　 *He pulls hard. Opens it.*
　 　 *Weather.*
　 　 *He goes out.*

ROBERT.
ROBERT.

　 *His voice is drowned on the wind.*

**Ellen** He won't hear you.

**John** ROBERT.

**Ellen** There's nobody there.

　 *John re-enters.*

**John** Everywhere he goes he does this.
　 At Cambridge. In London.
　 He watches and he captures.
　 I drag along behind him.
　 You have him.
　 Rise with him.
　 Rise above and watch me disappear.
　 I try – I have been trying – to be decent.
　 But you go on – he goes on –
　 And I – And I – And I –
　 . . .
　 I can't do it.

**Ellen** What?

**John** I follow you around.
　 I'm like a damn dog at your heels.

**Ellen** What can't you do?

**John** I can't.
I want to –
I'm sorry.

**Ellen** Do you want to hit me?

**John** Good God no.

**Ellen** You moved – like you were to hit me.

**John** I don't want to hit you.

**Ellen** Then what?

**John** I'm going to the bothy.
I'll sleep there tonight.
I think it's better.
Don't you?

**Ellen** Why?

**John** Go with Robert. Go with Robert if you must.
Just don't make me witness it.

**Ellen** We're on the island.
Amongst birds, and rock, and water.
This is not London.
You talk about me as though I'm from a twopenny novel.
I'm flesh.
Look at me.
I like you, John.

**John** I see.

**Ellen** I want you.

**John** You want me?

**Ellen** Yes.

**John** And him?

97

**Ellen**  Yes.

**John**  That's monstrous.

**Ellen**  I am monstrous, then.

**John**  He is. He's monstrous. He's planted this . . .
You want me?

**Ellen**  I said so.
Is that monstrous?

**John**  Well. No.

**Ellen**  I'll go to the bothy.
I'll sleep there.
I should never have spoken.

**John**  Surely you can choose between us.

**Ellen**  I don't want to.

**John**  What – what – it's – what are you suggesting?

**Ellen**  I want you to touch me.
Here's my hand.
Hold it.

**John**  He'll come back.

**Ellen**  Quiet.
Take the water off the table.
Bring the blanket.
Put the blanket on the table.
Now come by the fire.
Stand in the warm, in front of me.
Look.

*She undresses.*
*Her clothes fall to the floor.*
*She laughs.*

**John**  What's funny.

**Ellen**  You look afraid.

**John**  I am.

**Ellen**  Take off your clothes.
Take me to the table.
We'll lie on the blanket.
I'm cold.
Warm me.

*They move to the table.*

**John**  Look – before – I ought to say –

**Ellen**  Shut up.

**John**  So that you know.
Before we –
That I do – love – my intentions –

**Ellen**  Birds and rock and water and us.
We're on the island.
No need of intentions here.

**John**  Right.

**Ellen**  Right.

*A moment of touching.
Kissing.
Suddenly.
A kicking at the door.*

**John**  Oh my God, he's come back.

**Ellen**  Stay.
Let him come.

*The door kicked open.
Wind and weather.*

**Robert**  They still fly, Johnny. I've been watching them.
In the storm. They still fly – it's as if they're part of it.

**John**  Robert, I – it's – I –

*Robert takes in the scene.*
*Robert shuts the door.*

**Ellen**  It's fine.
Let him sit by the fire.

**John**  I know it seems a bit rum.

**Ellen**  Look at him.

**John**  Robert, I can explain . . .

**Ellen**  Quiet.
Let it be dark.
Let him be silent.
Let me see him seeing us.

**John**  Robert, I – look, it's a bit awkward.
I do wish you'd say something.
Ellen and I – we – she –

**Ellen**  Put your hand on my breast.
Leave it there.
Feel my breathing.

**John**  Breathing –
I –

**Ellen**  Slowly.

**John**  I can't, I – stop.

**Ellen**  If you're going to make a fuss about it, then stop.

**John**  No. I . . .

**Ellen**  Go to the bothy.
Sleep there.
If you want to bring decency back to me.
Go.
Take yourself away.

**John** No, I want to. I want –

**Ellen** Then stay.

**John** It's just a bit – off-putting – having a spectator.
On a chap's first time.

**Ellen** Look at him.
Like a gull.
On his haunches.
Watching.

*A crash of thunder, lightning from the storm.*

**John** We're going to be struck by bloody lightning.

**Ellen** We're caught in his gaze, boy.
This bird's look.
Gull Robert-watching.
Drawing us into his gull eyes.
Into his gull mind till.
I'm watching myself.
Watching me and you.
Let me take you in.
Look at your white seal skin.
Like film stars we are, boy.
Made film star by his gull eyes.
Dark.
Light flickering.
The falling away of all things.
Gone from ourselves.
In a pagan place.
Under the eyes of the gull.

*A moment.*
*Their bodies perfect.*

**John** Robert.

**Robert** Notice it, Johnny. Remember.
Remember the surprise of her body.
Remember very precisely the heat of her breath.

The heat of her.
Which is life, remember, Johnny.
Life.
Life contains heat which you only notice when you touch.
When you stop hovering.
When you fall.

*Perhaps Robert is weeping.*

**John** This can't be, Robert.
It can't be.
You know that.
The boat will come.
It has to end.

**Robert** Does it?

*John pushes Ellen from him.*
*Rises from the table.*
*Covers himself.*

**Ellen** We'll send the boat away.
We'll stay.
I'll not go back.

**Robert** I've been watching the petrels, Johnny.
Watching them in the storm.
And I saw something.
They allow themselves to be taken.
They're drawn on currents of air and currents of water. They throw themselves into the storm and allow themselves to be taken.
Where d'you think they go, Johnny?
They land on the island, but they don't live on it.
It's a landfall but it's not their home.
They live unweighted by mainland, tethered only to an outlier.
Imagine.
Living without time.

Because time, Johnny, time belongs to the land.
Not to the sea and the air.
Imagine entering their world.
Imagine that.
No beginnings and no endings.
Limitless.
Imagine departing from the land.

**John** It can't be.

*A moment between the two boys.*
*Calmly, Robert walks out into the storm.*

**Ellen** Bring him back.

**John** Leave him.

**Ellen** He was weeping.

*Ellen goes to the door.*

**John** He's wet from the storm, it's rainwater, that's all.

*Dawn.*
*The sea crashing against rocks.*
*Thousands of seabirds.*
*Wind.*
*A bird rising.*
*A bird flying.*

### EIGHT

*Some weeks later.*
*Inside the chapel.*
*Ellen is looking at the candle box.*
*The door is kicked open by the Captain.*
*Ellen and John enter with him.*

**Captain** Bloody door.
You mean to say, lad, you were on this island for a
month and you never got round to fixing the door?

**John** Sorry, sir.

**Captain** No need to be sorry.
  It's your lookout.

**John** The stones seemed to shift.

**Captain** I daresay they did.

**Ellen** I've gathered my things, sir, from the bothy.
  Shall I take them to the boat?

**Captain** Leave them there.
  I'll have one of the chaps take them down to the beach.
  Can't have a lady carrying loads, can we?

**John** No, sir.

**Ellen** He's big now, John.
  Number One.
  He's grown.

**John** One of the birds, sir.
  Ellen's sort of adopted him.

**Captain** A pet.

**Ellen** He'll be flying soon.

**John** They migrate.

**Captain** Fascinating.
  Well, if you're all packed up.

**John** Ready as we'll ever be.

**Captain** You can get yourselves down to the launch.
  Quick as you can if you don't mind.
  I'd like to be sailing soon.

**Ellen** Is it all right, Captain.
  If I take a moment to say goodbye.
  To my uncle.

**Captain** Ah, yes . . . yes . . . right-ho. You do that.

**Ellen** Thank you.

**Captain** Poor girl.

**John** She's been a brick, sir.
A real brick.

**Captain** They're made of stern stuff.
Women here.
Bred in the bone.
I have a theory that it's the puffin.
I take it you ate puffin.

**John** I did, sir.

**Captain** Rank. Isn't it?

**John** Chicken cooked in axle-grease.

**Captain** Food on board. Cook'll sort you out for a roast-beef dinner.
You deserve it.
Still, you seem to have made yourself quite at home.
'The chapel', you said.

**John** That's what the shepherds call it.

**Captain** Poor-looking chapel.
No doubt he was a poor-looking priest.
Have you boxed up all your documents?

**John** Yes, sir.
All the survey notes.
Photographs.
All there.

**Captain** The ministry chaps are eager to see what you've got.
Whether the island is suitable for the project.
I have to say, it looks ideal to me.

**John** I think it will be suitable, sir. Pristine. A diamond.

**Captain**  Now listen,
  Before we go.
  About the other lad.

**John**  Robert, sir.

**Captain**  Robert, yes.

**John**  Fell, sir.

**Captain**  So you said.

  *At the cliff top, Ellen stands, looking out to sea.*

**Ellen**  When it was over.
  He walked out into the storm and I followed him
because he seemed to have been weeping.

**John**  He was in the habit of swimming.
  In the morning.
  He would swim.

**Ellen**  Into the dawn he walked. Up the hill he walked.
  To the cliff top.

**John**  I thought he can't be going to do that.
  Not now.
  Not in a storm.

**Ellen**  And he made a short run.

**John**  I feel just awful about the whole thing.

**Ellen**  He ran at the cliff edge
  And spread his arms out and flew.

**John**  It was typical of him.
  Not thinking.
  The complete absence of questions.

**Ellen**  He flew.

**John**  By the time we got down to the rocks on the
shoreline, the storm had taken his body away.

**Ellen**  Away, away. Far out to sea.

**Captain**  Careless.

**John**  Yes, sir.

**Captain**  Cliffs.
  Always a gamble.

**John**  I should have done something.

**Captain**  Not your fault.
  He was the senior.

**John**  About Robert, sir.

**Captain**  We'll need a report, of course.

**John**  He – I wondered – telling his parents.

**Captain**  Ministry'll see to all that.

**John**  Right.

**Captain**  Come on then. Ship's waiting. Let's get a move on.
  Take the stuff down to the beach.
  Where's the girl?

**John**  I'll fetch her.

**Captain**  Right-ho.

**John**  Captain, would you mind, since the island's going to be – well – out of commission shall we say . . .?
  Would you mind – is there room for the table?

**Captain**  The table?

**John**  Yes. It's a couple of hundred years old I think.
  A souvenir if you like.
  And besides.
  Just to have it sitting here while the whole island around it is incapable of supporting life.
  Seems an awful waste of a table.

**Captain** Of course.
 If you put it like that.
 I'll mention it to the chaps.
 Have them bring it down with the rest of the gear.
 Right-ho.
 Back to civilisation.

 *He tries to shut the door.*

Can't shut the bloody door.

**John** Doesn't bloody matter now does it?
 Excuse my French.

 *The Captain and John walk away from the chapel.*
  *A fork-tail calling in the corner of the chapel.*

 *The End.*